Welcome to a heartfelt a journey through the grips of addiction obsession with gaming. Within these pages, I aim to provide a candid exploration of my personal experiences, offering insights and lessons that can illuminate the struggles and challenges faced by both gamers and their loved ones.

Gaming addiction can be a deeply isolating and perplexing battle, often misunderstood by those who haven't experienced it firsthand. Through my own story, I hope to shed light on the intricate web of emotions, thoughts, and behaviors that come hand in hand with this addiction. By sharing my vulnerabilities and triumphs, I aspire to create a bridge of understanding between gamers and their close ones, fostering empathy and compassion.

This book is not solely meant for individuals grappling with addiction; it is also intended for those who may not recognize the profound impact our daily habits can have on ourselves and the people around us. In our fast-paced, technology-driven world, it is easy to become oblivious to the subtle ways in which our choices influence our relationships, mental well-being, and overall quality of life. By delving into the intricacies of my addiction, I hope to awaken readers to the significance of mindful self-reflection and the importance of recognizing when our behaviors veer into unhealthy territory.

Throughout this narrative, I will recount the trials and tribulations of my addiction, describing the all-consuming allure of virtual worlds and the toll they took on my physical and mental health. I will not shy away from the darker aspects of my journey, addressing the moments of despair, self-doubt, and the detrimental impact on my relationships. However, woven within these somber threads are also tales of resilience, personal growth, and the unwavering determination to reclaim my life from the clutches of addiction.

Above all, my intention is to inspire hope and foster a sense of community among those impacted by gaming addiction. By sharing my story, I hope to convey the message that recovery is possible, that transformation and healing are within reach, and that no one needs to face this battle alone. Together, we can illuminate the path to recovery, strengthen relationships, and create a future where gaming can be enjoyed responsibly, without sacrificing our well-being and the connections that truly matter.

Join me on this profound and enlightening journey, as we delve deep into the heart of gaming addiction, shedding light on its shadows and uncovering the keys to reclaiming our lives and building a brighter, more balanced future.

I firmly believe that the journey of addiction, whether it be to video games or any other form, does not define our worth as individuals. It is neither a mark of superiority nor an indicator of inferiority compared to those who have never experienced such struggles. We are all unique beings with diverse paths, and it is through these experiences, including our triumphs and challenges, that we shape our identities.

Instead of harboring sadness or anger about my past struggles with gaming addiction, I have come to embrace them as an integral part of my life's narrative. They have contributed to the person I am today, instilling in me a profound sense of empathy, resilience, and an unwavering determination to overcome obstacles. Recognizing the significance of self-acceptance, I have chosen not to dwell in regret or self-blame, but rather to channel my energy towards personal growth.

If there are aspects of myself that I am dissatisfied with at this moment, I acknowledge that it is within my power to take proactive steps towards positive transformation. Every day presents an opportunity for the conscious decision to embark on a journey to better myself. It is a journey that requires courage, perseverance, and a willingness to confront the shadows within ourselves.

In extending an invitation to you, dear reader, I implore you to join me on this transformative path. Embrace your own unique struggles, whether they be related to addiction or other challenges, and recognize that they do not define your worth. By embarking on a quest for personal betterment, you open the door to a world of possibility—a realm where growth, healing, and self-discovery intertwine.

Let us collectively embark on a voyage towards self-compassion. Embrace the potential within yourself, for it is through nurturing our own well-being that we can inspire positive change in others. Together, we can foster a community built upon understanding and mutual growth.

Are there areas of your life that you aspire to improve? Are there patterns or behaviors that no longer serve you? Embrace the notion that you have the power to shape your own destiny, to break free from your shackles.

Remember, it is not about comparing ourselves to others or seeking external validation. Rather, it is a profound act of self-love and self-compassion. Embrace the opportunity for growth, and together, let us walk hand in hand towards a better you.

Chapter 1: Introduction

As we embark on this journey together, I invite you to join me in exploring the depths of my personal transformation. Hi, my name is James, and I find myself entangled in the clutches of an addiction that revolves around the captivating world of video games.

As I stand before you, I cannot claim to be an expert on the terminology that surrounds addiction. Labels such as "recovering addict" or "recovered addict" may carry different connotations for different individuals. What I can confidently assert, however, is that I reached a point in my life where my time spent playing video games far exceeded what I would like to admit.

Acknowledging the depth of my addiction was a pivotal moment that opened the doors to a minefield. It required a candid examination of my choices, habits, and the impact they had on my overall well-being and the relationships that mattered most to me. In doing so, I confronted the need for change and embarked on a transformative journey toward a healthier and more balanced existence.

My story is not one of despair or hopelessness. Rather, it is a testament to the power of self-awareness and the determination to overcome the challenges that lie in our path. Throughout this conversation, I aim to share the insights and lessons I have gleaned from my own experiences, with the hope that they may resonate with others who find themselves on a similar journey.

Video games, with their immersive worlds and compelling narratives, have an undeniable allure. They offer an escape from daily life, providing a sense of achievement and excitement. However, like any passion, when indulged in to an excessive extent, it can tip the balance and impede our ambitions and well being.

Recognizing the impact my addiction had on my life was a humbling experience. It illuminated the moments I missed with loved ones, the opportunities I neglected, and the toll it took on my mental well-being. However, dwelling on regret or self-pity would have hindered my progress. Instead, I chose to focus on the present and the steps I needed to take to reclaim my life.

So, as we delve deeper into this discussion, I encourage you to reflect on your own relationship with video games or any other passion that may have consumed your time and energy. Are there aspects of your life that you feel could be more balanced? What steps can you take to align your passions with your overall well-being?

Remember, this is not a journey to be taken alone. Together, we can support and inspire one another, celebrating the victories and offering solace during the moments of doubt. The path to a healthier existence is within your grasp, and with an open heart and mind, you can claw back some control into your life.

Allow me to take you on a nostalgic journey into the roots of my gaming addiction. As I reflect upon my earliest memories, I find myself transported back to a time when gaming was not only a source of joy but also an opportunity for self-discovery and perseverance.

Alotho this might find this section of this book less pertinent, i invite you to reflect on the place that gaming or your obsessing has in your life. And more importantly how it sipped into this position in your life. Reflecting and discovering the source of your addiction might lead you to understand the parts of your mind that need healing.

It all began with a humble download of Warcraft III on our family computer—an experience that would shape my gaming habits for years to come. As the eldest sibling in a household where my parents weren't particularly inclined towards technology, I found myself assuming the role of a self-taught enthusiast. The task at hand, though seemingly trivial now, posed a significant challenge for a young James.

With determination and curiosity as my guiding forces, I embarked on a quest to install the game and unlock the vast world that awaited me. It required patience, trial and error, and a deep willingness to explore the realm of technology. As I overcame each obstacle, whether it was deciphering unfamiliar technical jargon or troubleshooting unforeseen issues, a sense of accomplishment coursed through my veins.

Little did I know that this initial step into the world of gaming would mark the beginning of a profound journey—one that would intertwine with my life's experiences and shape my identity. Through the challenges and triumphs encountered in those early gaming endeavors, I began to develop vital skills such as problem-solving, critical thinking, and adaptability.

The world of gaming became a canvas upon which I painted the brushstrokes of my identity. It offered a space where I could explore, experiment, and unravel the depths of my own potential. It was in those virtual realms that I discovered the joy of creativity, the power of imagination, and the exhilaration of pushing beyond perceived limitations.

Looking back, I am grateful for the opportunities gaming provided in nurturing my personal growth. It ignited a flame within me, propelling me to seek knowledge, develop new skills, and embrace the ever-evolving landscape of technology. These early experiences shaped not only my gaming habits but also my approach to challenges in the real world.

So, as I share this part of my journey with you, I encourage you to reflect on your own early experiences with gaming or any other passion that captivated your heart. How did those moments shape your character? What skills did you acquire? And how have those lessons influenced your outlook on life?

Embrace the nostalgia and let it guide you on a path of self-discovery. For within those cherished memories lie the seeds, waiting to be nurtured and bloom into a future filled with possibility and resilience.

As my journey through the world of gaming progressed, I found myself exploring new platforms and immersing myself in a variety of captivating experiences. From the Gameboy Advance to the Xbox 360, each console became a portal to different realms, where I could unleash my imagination and embark on unforgettable adventures.

After delving into the intricacies of Warcraft III on the family computer, I sought out new gaming experiences that would fuel my passion further. Enter the Gameboy Advance, a handheld console that became my constant companion. With the iconic Pokemon Red variant in hand, I embarked on a captivating journey through the enchanting world of pocket monsters. The allure of capturing, training, and battling these creatures proved irresistible, captivating me for hours on end.

The Gameboy Advance offered a unique sense of portability and convenience, allowing me to embark on gaming adventures wherever I went. Whether I was waiting for the school bus, on family trips, or simply seeking solace in my own little world, the Gameboy Advance served as a gateway to realms teeming with endless possibilities.

As time went on and technology continued to evolve, my appetite for gaming grew. The Xbox 360 emerged as the next chapter in my gaming odyssey, offering a wealth of titles that catered to every genre and interest. It became my ultimate source of entertainment, granting me access to a vast library of games that expanded my horizons.

I eagerly explored a myriad of genres, from action-packed adventures to immersive role-playing epics and thrilling first-person shooters. The Xbox 360 became a gateway to uncharted worlds and virtual landscapes, where I could lose myself in compelling narratives, awe-inspiring visuals, and adrenaline-pumping gameplay.

Every game that fell into my hands became an opportunity for discovery, a chance to unravel new stories and test my skills. With iconic franchises like Halo that pushed the boundaries of creativity, I embraced a diverse range of gaming experiences that enriched my understanding of storytelling, teamwork, and the limitless possibilities of interactive entertainment.

As I ventured into my teenage years, my passion for gaming reached new heights, driven by the introduction of an IMac into our family household. It was during this pivotal time that I embarked on a gaming journey that would leave an indelible mark on my life.

At the age of 14, armed with curiosity and a yearning for immersive experiences, I took my first steps into the realm of "real" gaming. The game that captured my attention and ignited my imagination was none other than Minecraft. In those early days, it was still in its alpha or beta stage, yet its potential was already evident.

Equipped with an IMac that possessed modest specifications, I dove headfirst into the blocky world of Minecraft, embracing its endless possibilities and boundless creativity. Although my gaming setup offered a meager 24 frames per second and lacked the bells and whistles of a high-end system, it didn't dampen my enthusiasm. Instead, it fueled my determination to extract every ounce of joy from the experience.

Coincidentally, this phase of my gaming journey coincided with a significant change in my personal life. Our family had recently relocated to a rural town, where the hustle and bustle of city life were replaced by the serenity of nature. Finding myself distanced from familiar friends and social circles, gaming became my steadfast companion—a source of solace and excitement during those solitary moments.

In the virtual world of Minecraft, I discovered a sanctuary where I could build, explore, and unleash my creativity without limitations. The game's pixelated landscapes offered an escape from the isolation I felt in the real world, allowing me to forge my own adventures and shape a world that existed solely in my imagination.

As the summer sun cast its warm glow upon the world, a determined fire burned within me. I embarked on a mission to transform my gaming aspirations into a tangible reality, fueled by the prospect of owning my very first gaming setup. It was a time of hard work, of laboring under the summer heat to save every precious penny.
With each passing day, as I toiled away at various jobs, the vision of my gaming sanctuary grew clearer in my mind. I didn't seek opulence or extravagance, but rather a humble collection of components that would bring me closer to the virtual worlds I held dear.

When the end of summer finally arrived, I stood on the precipice of fulfillment. With my hard-earned savings in hand, I set out to buy my first gaming setup. It was a journey that required careful consideration and deliberate choices, but one that I approached with a mixture of excitement and caution.

A comfortable chair became the foundation upon which my gaming adventures would unfold. Patiently sifting through options until I found a seat that promised respite during long gaming sessions. It may not have been the most luxurious of chairs, but it held within it the promise of countless hours of immersion and joy.

The peripherals—keyboard and mouse—became my loyal companions in the digital realm. I hunted for bargains, determined to find the perfect balance between affordability and functionality. Each key press and mouse click would carry me deeper into the realms of fantasy, guided by the tools I had carefully chosen.

A monitor, though not the most cutting-edge, became my window into breathtaking digital landscapes. I sought one that would faithfully render the vibrant colors and detailed textures of the virtual worlds I yearned to explore. As I powered it on for the first time, the display flickered to life, hinting at the grand adventures that awaited me.

And then there was the centerpiece—the PC itself. While it may not have boasted the latest and greatest specifications, it held a special place in my heart. It was a modest machine.This humble contraption would serve as the conduit for countless hours of entertainment.

With my newly acquired gaming setup, I felt an exhilarating sense of liberation. No longer bound by the limitations of borrowed consoles or outdated technology, I could finally immerse myself in a proper gaming experience. It was as if a whole new world had opened its doors to me, brimming with endless possibilities and thrilling adventures.

To my delight, my best friend had also managed to procure his own gaming setup. We were united by our shared passion, forming an unbreakable bond that would carry us through countless virtual escapades. Together, we delved into the realms of fantasy and competition, forging unforgettable memories that would shape our friendship for years to come.

From that moment forward, gaming became an integral part of my daily routine. It was a ritual that held both comfort and excitement, a sanctuary where I could lose myself in captivating narratives and engage in fierce battles against virtual adversaries. The world around me could fade into the background as I embarked on epic quests, solved intricate puzzles, or honed my skills in competitive arenas.

Days turned into weeks, and weeks into months, yet my enthusiasm for gaming remained unwavering. Each day held the promise of new adventures, undiscovered worlds, and the thrill of unlocking achievements. It became a part of my identity, a source of solace and exhilaration in a world that often seemed chaotic and unpredictable.

Of course, there were moments when life demanded my attention, forcing me to temporarily set aside my gaming pursuits. Responsibilities, obligations, and unforeseen circumstances occasionally interrupted my gaming sessions, causing a brief pause in my digital escapades. But even during those brief hiatuses, my mind yearned for the moment when I could once again pick up the controller or sit before my keyboard, ready to delve back into the virtual realms I had come to adore.

As the years rolled by and I matured, my gaming preferences began to evolve. The allure of competitive gaming beckoned to me, drawing me into a world of adrenaline-pumping challenges and thrilling rivalries. It was during this phase that I discovered the captivating realms of League of Legends, Rocket League, and the ever-engrossing time sink that is Old School RuneScape.

League of Legends, with its strategic depth and intense team dynamics, captured my attention like no other. The rush of coordinating with teammates, executing well-planned strategies, and outmaneuvering opponents ignited a competitive fire within me. Each match was an opportunity to showcase my skills, communicate with teammates, and strive for victory. From the epic clashes on the Summoner's Rift to the meticulous decision-making in drafting champions, League of Legends became a battleground where friendships were forged and rivalries were kindled.

Rocket League, on the other hand, offered a different kind of thrill—a fusion of soccer and high-speed vehicular acrobatics. The rush of launching into the air, performing aerial maneuvers, and executing precise shots filled each match with heart-pounding excitement. Whether playing solo or in a team, Rocket League rewarded quick reflexes, precise control, and impeccable coordination. It was a game that required both finesse and strategic positioning, as each goal celebrated or deflated the hopes of victory.

And then there was the enchanting world of Old School RuneScape, a nostalgic journey back to the golden age of MMORPGs. In this sprawling virtual realm, I found myself engrossed in a vast tapestry of quests, exploration, and character progression. Hours upon hours were devoted to embarking on perilous adventures, delving into treacherous dungeons, and honing my skills in combat and various trades. Old School RuneScape captivated me not only with its addictive gameplay but also with its sense of community, as I interacted with fellow players and embarked on epic quests together.

Navigating the intricate landscape of my mental health has been a lifelong journey, one filled with challenges and triumphs. Even from a tender age, the shadows of depression and anxiety cast their gloom upon my young spirit. The weight of these emotional burdens often felt overwhelming, shaping the way I perceived the world and interacted with those around me.

To compound these struggles, the presence of dyslexia and attention deficit disorder added an extra layer of complexity to my academic experiences. School, a place meant to foster growth and learning, became a battleground where my self-esteem took blows and my confidence waned. Reading difficulties and a propensity for distraction made it arduous to keep up with the demands of traditional education, further exacerbating my feelings of frustration and inadequacy.

However, amidst the tumultuous waves of my mental health challenges, gaming emerged as an unexpected source of solace and empowerment. In the virtual worlds I explored, my dyslexia and attention deficit disorder held no sway. There, I could immerse myself in captivating narratives, engage in strategic gameplay, and forge meaningful connections with like-minded individuals who shared my passion.

Gaming, in its own unique way, had become my sanctuary, a cherished abode where I sought refuge from the judgment and pressures of the outside world. Within its digital realms, I discovered solace and solitude, a respite from the constant scrutiny and expectations that weighed upon me. It was a space where I could retreat into myself, free from the prying eyes and critical voices that often infiltrated my daily life.

One of the aspects that drew me deeper into the realm of gaming was the unparalleled sense of control it offered. Every aspect of my gaming experience could be customized and tailored to my liking. From character creation to gameplay preferences, I held the reins of my virtual universe. It was a realm where I could shape my own destiny, forge my own path, and dictate the outcomes of my virtual adventures.

In a world that often felt chaotic and unpredictable, this ability to exert control over my gaming environment was both empowering and cathartic. It allowed me to navigate challenges on my own terms, conquering obstacles and emerging victorious. The sense of mastery and agency I derived from gaming provided a counterbalance to the perceived lack of control I experienced in other aspects of my life.

Beyond the realm of personal customization, gaming also offered a playground for my creativity to flourish. Whether it was building intricate structures in sandbox games or designing unique strategies in competitive multiplayer arenas, I reveled in the opportunity to express my imaginative ideas and witness them come to life. Gaming became a canvas upon which I could unleash my creativity, unhindered by the limitations of the physical world.

And yet, as comforting as the world of gaming was for me, it became a double-edged sword. The very sense of relaxation and detachment that initially drew me in also fueled the unhealthy spiral of my habits. I found myself increasingly consumed by the virtual realms, losing track of time and neglecting other aspects of my life. What began as a harmless escape gradually morphed into a destructive pattern.

In those final months before I made the decision to quit gaming cold turkey, the consequences of my excessive habits began to manifest in unsettling ways. Neglected responsibilities piled up, relationships suffered, and my overall well-being deteriorated. The once-engaging pastime had transformed into an all-encompassing obsession that held me captive, blinding me to the toll it was taking on my life.

I vividly remember the internal turmoil I experienced during that period. A part of me recognized the detrimental impact of my gaming addiction, yet another part was hesitant to let go of the comforting familiarity it provided. It was a battle between acknowledging the need for change and succumbing to the solace I had found for so long.

The realization of the unhealthy state of affairs did not come easily. It required a moment of clarity, a jarring wake-up call that shook me from my complacency. I saw the toll it was taking on my physical and mental well-being, the strain it placed on my relationships, and the missed opportunities that passed me by while I remained immersed in pixels and pixels alone.

With a heavy heart and a determined spirit, I made the difficult decision to break free from the grip of my gaming addiction. It was not a choice made lightly, but one that was necessary for my own growth, healing, and reclaiming of a balanced life. I knew that in order to nurture my mental health, mend fractured connections, and rediscover my passions, I had to sever the ties that held me captive in the virtual realm.

Quitting gaming cold turkey was no easy feat. It required immense discipline, resilience, and a support system to lean on during moments of temptation. I sought solace in the company of loved ones, engaging in activities that reminded me of the joy of the offline world. I explored new hobbies, rekindled old passions, and discovered the beauty of genuine human connections that extended beyond the confines of a screen.

While the journey to break free from my gaming addiction was undoubtedly challenging, it was also a catalyst for self-discovery. It opened my eyes to the importance of finding a healthy balance in life, where digital entertainment could coexist harmoniously with other fulfilling endeavors. I learned to appreciate the value of moderation, setting boundaries, and prioritizing my well-being.

Acknowledging the depths to which I had sunk was a painful yet necessary step towards my recovery. It required a moment of self-reflection, a realization that the virtual world, while captivating and enticing, could not replace the fulfillment and richness that the real world had to offer. I yearned for a life beyond the confines of the screen, one that embraced meaningful connections, personal growth, and a balanced existence.

The impact that excessive gaming had on my life

The insidious nature of excessive gaming and gaming addiction crept into my life with a subtle yet undeniable force. Looking back, I realize that the impacts were far from minor, but in my state of denial, I failed to recognize the extent of their reach. I clung to a false sense of control, convincing myself that I had mastery over my gaming habits when, in reality, they had consumed me entirely.

At the onset, it seemed harmless. I would lose myself in the virtual realms, engrossed in the exhilaration of each gaming session. Time seemed to slip away unnoticed as I chased the next achievement, conquered new levels, and immersed myself in digital adventures. The world outside my gaming bubble faded into the background, eclipsed by the allure of pixels and virtual conquests.

Yet, beneath the surface of my seemingly controlled facade, the consequences began to pile up. Relationships strained under the weight of my preoccupation, as I withdrew from the real-world connections that once brought joy and fulfillment. Responsibilities and obligations were pushed aside, their significance diminished in the face of my insatiable gaming appetite.

The subtle signs of addiction began to emerge, like cracks in the foundation of my self-perception. I experienced restlessness and irritability when I was unable to play, a persistent longing that gnawed at my consciousness. The world beyond the screen began to lose its luster, fading into insignificance compared to the simulated reality I had created for myself.

Despite the mounting evidence of my lack of control, I clung to the illusion of mastery. I dismissed the concerns of loved ones, brushing off their observations as exaggerations or misunderstandings. Deep down, however, a part of me knew the truth. I was trapped in a web of dependency, unable to break free from the grip of gaming addiction.

The grip of gaming addiction tightened its hold on my life, manifesting primarily in the realm of my mental health. A subtle shift occurred, as my gaming habits transformed from a source of joy and entertainment into a pressing and compulsive need to play. It became an all-consuming force, eclipsing other aspects of my life and distorting my perception of what truly mattered.

The pressures and demands of the gaming world took precedence over everything else. My thoughts were constantly occupied by strategies, quests, and virtual achievements. The boundary between my digital existence and the real world blurred, as I prioritized the fabricated challenges and rewards of gaming over the tangible experiences and responsibilities of daily life.

Sleep, once a restorative and rejuvenating activity, became a casualty of my addiction. Nights bled into mornings as I succumbed to the allure of virtual conquests. I would find myself awake until the early hours, fueling my obsession with games until exhaustion overcame me. But even then, I justified my sleep deprivation, convincing myself that it was a testament to my passion rather than a red flag of addiction.

Denial became my shield, deflecting any suggestion that I was ensnared in the clutches of gaming addiction. I refused to acknowledge the signs, dismissing concerns from loved ones and rejecting the notion that my behavior was anything but a genuine love for what I did. The more others expressed worry, the more steadfastly I clung to my conviction that my excessive gaming was a testament to my dedication and enjoyment.

However, as time went on, the cracks in my façade began to deepen. The toll on my mental health became increasingly apparent. The pressures that once seemed exhilarating now weighed heavily on my psyche, feeding into a relentless cycle of compulsion and self-imposed expectations. The highs of virtual victories were short-lived, quickly replaced by a desperate need for the next fix, driving me deeper into the addictive spiral.

Amidst the grip of my gaming addiction, a bittersweet truth emerged—I did find enjoyment in my extensive gaming sessions, at least on the surface. There were moments of exhilaration, camaraderie with fellow gamers, and the thrill of conquering virtual worlds. However, beneath this veneer of enjoyment, a deep dissatisfaction gnawed at my soul.

As a creative individual, I possessed a rich tapestry of passions and interests that had once defined my identity. Visual arts, writing, reading—they had been the conduits through which I expressed my innermost thoughts and emotions. Cooking, a culinary symphony of flavors and experimentation, had brought me immense pleasure. Engaging in intellectual debates and exploring ideas had fueled the fire of my curiosity.

Yet, the voracious appetite of my gaming addiction had swallowed these vibrant aspects of my life whole. The more I immersed myself in virtual realms, the more the other facets of my being faded into obscurity. They became mere echoes of a time when I had pursued them with zeal and enthusiasm.

I mourned the loss of my creative outlets and intellectual pursuits, feeling a profound emptiness that gaming could not fill. The hours spent gaming, while momentarily gratifying, left me yearning for a deeper sense of purpose and fulfillment. I longed to reconnect with the parts of myself that had been silenced, to rediscover the joy and satisfaction that flowed from expressing my creativity and engaging in thought-provoking conversations.

From the moment I entered into a relationship seven years ago, my commitment was clear—I would prioritize my girlfriend above all else. It was a promise I made to myself, a testament to the depth of my love and devotion. However, unbeknownst to me, my dedication had gradually eroded beneath the weight of my gaming addiction. It was only when I finally broke free from the clutches of gaming that I realized how far I had strayed from being the partner I aspired to be.

In the grip of my obsession, my thoughts became clouded, my focus diverted. Gaming held a powerful sway over my mind, consuming my every waking thought and blurring the lines between the virtual and the real. Unbeknownst to me, this insidious influence had seeped into the very fabric of my relationship, casting a shadow over the love and commitment I professed.

Guilt washed over me as I examined the moments I had missed, the opportunities for connection I had overlooked. The intimacy and emotional closeness that had once defined our bond had been compromised, replaced by a wall of indifference that I had unwittingly constructed. It was a painful reckoning—a realization that I had failed to be the partner I had always envisioned.

My beloved husky, a loyal and affectionate companion, held a special place in my heart. Our bond was forged through shared moments of playfulness, cuddles, and heartfelt interactions. However, as my gaming addiction consumed my life, even this cherished connection began to fade. I found myself neglecting the very source of unconditional love and joy that had always been present in my furry friend.

In the whirlwind of my gaming obsession, the mornings that were once dedicated to my husky transformed into a mere fleeting interaction. I would hurriedly greet her, barely sparing a moment for affection before rushing back to the beckoning glow of my computer screen. Time once spent in her company, engaging in play and showering her with attention, was now replaced by the urgency to return to my virtual adventures.

The realization of how my gaming addiction had impacted my relationship with my mother struck me with a mix of emotions. As someone who values openness and close connections within my family, hearing her perspective on the transformation that occurred within me was both shocking and eye-opening.

Living under the same roof, my mother had witnessed firsthand the subtle but significant changes that had taken hold of my being during the height of my gaming obsession. She had seen glimpses of her once vibrant and animated child fade into the backdrop of virtual realms, consumed by the allure of pixels and endless gameplay.

Yet, as I embarked on my journey towards recovery, the transformation that unfolded within me did not go unnoticed. It was as if a veil had been lifted, revealing the essence of who I truly was—a person filled with life, enthusiasm, and an eagerness to engage with the world beyond the confines of a virtual screen.

My mother's heartfelt words resonated deeply within me. It was a testament to the power of change and the resilience of our bond. She expressed how she felt as though she had "gotten her kid back," emphasizing the stark contrast between the diminished version of myself that had been consumed by the virtual world and the revitalized individual who stood before her.

I want to emphasize a crucial point: I hold no animosity towards video games. It would be all too easy to succumb to anger and place the blame solely on this form of entertainment. There may even be a temptation to ban or prohibit them altogether. However, I firmly believe that such extreme measures are not justified or necessary.

I cannot deny the significance of video games in my life. Some of my fondest memories revolve around the joyous moments spent playing alongside friends, embarking on epic adventures and engaging in friendly competition. These experiences have left an indelible mark on my personal journey, contributing to the person I am today.

It is through gaming that I honed my ability to teach myself new skills and knowledge. The interactive nature of games encouraged me to think critically, strategize, and adapt to ever-changing scenarios. These invaluable attributes have transcended the virtual realm, permeating into various aspects of my life. The capacity to navigate complex challenges, analyze information, and make informed decisions has proven indispensable in both personal and professional endeavors.

Rather than demonizing video games, it is essential to recognize the positive aspects they offer. Like any form of entertainment, moderation and balance are key. It is when gaming becomes an obsession, overshadowing other important aspects of life, that it can have detrimental effects.

I advocate for a mindful and responsible approach to gaming, one that allows for enjoyment and growth while maintaining a healthy equilibrium. By setting boundaries, prioritizing other interests and responsibilities, and fostering a diverse range of experiences, we can harness the benefits of gaming while avoiding the pitfalls of addiction.

The key lies in self-awareness and self-discipline. Understanding our own tendencies and vulnerabilities enables us to strike a harmonious balance between the virtual world and the realities of everyday life. It is essential to cultivate a sense of agency and autonomy, ensuring that our choices and actions are guided by our own desires rather than being dictated by external forces.

I encourage individuals to explore the multifaceted nature of their passions and hobbies, allowing them to shape and enrich their lives rather than dominating their existence. Let us embrace the positive aspects of gaming while nurturing a holistic approach to personal growth, fostering relationships, and pursuing a diverse range of interests.

It is essential for me to acknowledge that no external factor is inherently good or bad. In the case of gaming, I firmly believe that the responsibility lies with me, rather than placing blame on the medium itself. It is a humbling realization that I lacked the necessary self-control and introspection to cultivate a healthy relationship with gaming.

Chapter 2:
The Problem with Digital Distraction

The ways in which technology and digital media can be addictive and distracting

In a world characterized by stress, judgment, and the complexities of everyday life, I found solace in the realm of gaming, YouTube, and other online media. These platforms became my means of escape from the realities I found challenging and disheartening.

Life can often feel overwhelming, with its myriad responsibilities, societal expectations, and personal struggles. It was during these moments of vulnerability that I sought refuge in the digital world. Gaming, with its immersive storytelling and interactive experiences, offered a temporary reprieve from the pressures and anxieties that weighed me down.

Similarly, YouTube and other online media platforms became an escape into a realm of curated content. With just a click, I could enter a world of diverse creators, captivating stories, and thought-provoking discussions. The ability to curate my own content consumption allowed me to tailor my online experiences to match my interests and preferences, further enhancing the sense of escape and disconnection from my everyday struggles.

While seeking refuge in these digital realms brought temporary relief, I now recognize that relying solely on escapism was not a sustainable or healthy approach. It became apparent that I needed to address the underlying issues that fueled my desire to escape in the first place.

In a world filled with distractions and instant gratification, it often feels easier to succumb to the allure of opening TikTok or indulging in a game of League of Legends than to face the daunting task of introspection, self-improvement, and personal growth. It's human nature to seek immediate comfort and pleasure, even if it means neglecting the deeper issues and responsibilities that require our attention.

Staring at our reflection in the mirror, both figuratively and literally, can be an uncomfortable experience. It forces us to confront our insecurities, our fears, and the aspects of ourselves that we wish to improve. It demands self-awareness and the willingness to challenge our own limitations. It requires us to be vulnerable and courageous in the face of change.

Similarly, dedicating time to study for an exam or engaging in physical exercise to improve our health can seem like arduous tasks. They require discipline, effort, and a willingness to prioritize long-term goals over short-term pleasures. The immediate gratification offered by digital entertainment often pales in comparison to the satisfaction and sense of accomplishment that comes from personal growth and self-improvement.

Games possess a unique ability to provide us with precisely calibrated challenges, ensuring that we encounter just enough resistance to make the eventual reward all the more satisfying. Their carefully crafted mechanics, captivating narratives, and immersive worlds are designed to captivate our attention and keep us engaged. In contrast, activities like going for a run can initially appear daunting and require us to overcome physical exertion, discomfort, and the natural resistance of our own bodies.

When comparing the allure of gaming to the prospect of going for a run, it's undeniable that games offer a seemingly effortless path to enjoyment. With their instant gratification and constant stimulation, they provide a readily accessible source of entertainment and pleasure. In the gaming realm, we can embark on epic adventures, conquer challenging quests, and experience a sense of accomplishment with each level-up or achievement unlocked.

On the other hand, going for a run demands physical effort, perseverance, and a willingness to push through initial resistance. It requires stepping outside our comfort zones, confronting the potential discomfort of physical exertion, and embracing the physical challenges that come with it. Unlike the seamless progression in a game, running may involve fatigue, sweat, and moments of doubt where the immediate rewards seem less apparent.

Indeed, one of the aspects that make gaming and social media so appealing is the inherent sense of structure and tangible progress they provide. In the digital realm, every action and achievement are neatly defined, measured, and rewarded. Whether it's gaining experience points, leveling up, or unlocking new abilities, the feedback loop in games creates a constant sense of growth and accomplishment.

When training cooking skills in a video game, the satisfaction of seeing your character's experience and levels increase is immediate and gratifying. It offers a clear sense of progress and a tangible representation of your culinary prowess within the game's virtual world. On the other hand, real-life activities such as running lack these explicit markers of achievement. There are no numerical values or experience points to quantify your progress or validate your efforts.

Running, in particular, can be an emotionally demanding activity. Unlike the virtual realm where positive chimes and notifications reinforce our achievements, the real-world experience of running can be much more nuanced and subjective. Instead of a cheery sound when running a faster mile, we are often left with our own internal assessments and perceptions. We might find ourselves comparing our current performance to past runs or setting personal goals, which can lead to feelings of disappointment or frustration if we perceive a decline in performance.

Moreover, external factors such as physical ailments, fatigue, or external stressors can impact our running experience. These factors can influence our performance and make it challenging to consistently achieve faster times or improved distances. It's natural to feel discouraged when facing obstacles that hinder our progress, even if they are justified and understandable.

However, it's important to shift our perspective and embrace a more holistic view of physical activities like running. Rather than solely focusing on immediate external rewards or measurable progress, we can find fulfillment and satisfaction in the inherent benefits of the activity itself. Running serves as an opportunity for self-reflection, personal growth, and a chance to disconnect from the digital world and reconnect with our physical selves.

Running is an organic, dynamic process that allows us to tune into our bodies, experience the rhythm of our breath, and engage with the world around us. It provides an avenue for introspection and an opportunity to challenge ourselves mentally and physically.

Instead of relying solely on external validation, we can cultivate an internal sense of achievement by setting personal goals and celebrating our progress, regardless of how it compares to previous runs or the achievements in the gaming world. By embracing the process and recognizing the intrinsic rewards of running —such as improved stamina, increased endurance, and enhanced mental well-being—we can find joy and fulfillment in our real-life experiences.

It's crucial to acknowledge that the allure of gaming and social media lies in their structured nature and immediate rewards. However, by embracing the uncertainties and challenges of real-life activities like running, we open ourselves up to a more authentic and meaningful connection with ourselves and the world around us. Running may not have the same auditory cues or quantifiable rewards, but it offers an opportunity for personal growth, resilience, and a deeper understanding of our own capabilities.

So, let us not underestimate the value of the intangible rewards that come with real-life activities. Let us embrace the complexities, the fluctuations, and the subjective nature of pursuits like running. By doing so, we can cultivate a healthier relationship with both the digital and physical realms, finding fulfillment and balance as we navigate the diverse landscapes of our lives.

The negative impact of digital distraction on mental health and wellbeing

The all-consuming nature of video game addiction undoubtedly had a significant impact on various aspects of my life. It created a relentless focus on gaming, making even mundane tasks seem like obstacles standing between me and my virtual adventures. The simple act of doing the dishes became a daunting chore, as my mind was constantly preoccupied with thoughts of what awaited me next in the world of RuneScape or other games.

However, the consequences of my addiction extended beyond household responsibilities. There were numerous challenges and difficulties I encountered as a result of my obsession with video games. Relationships with friends and family suffered, as I prioritized gaming over spending quality time with loved ones. I would decline invitations to social events or outings, opting to immerse myself in virtual worlds instead.

The addictive grip of gaming also affected my physical well-being. Neglecting basic self-care became the norm, as I would forgo necessary activities like going to the store or taking a walk in favor of maximizing my game time. The thought of stepping away from the screen seemed inconceivable because, in my mind, every minute not spent gaming felt like a missed opportunity for progression and achievement.

Reflecting on it now, I can see how I deluded myself into believing that my ability to stop gaming at any moment meant I wasn't truly addicted. I used this false notion as a shield to justify my excessive gaming habits. It was a way to avoid confronting the reality of my addiction and the negative impact it had on my life.

In truth, addiction is not solely defined by the inability to stop completely; it encompasses the obsessive thoughts, the compulsion to prioritize gaming over other essential activities, and the adverse consequences that arise from this behavior. My addiction had blinded me to the extent of its control over me, leading me to rationalize and downplay its impact.

Recognizing and acknowledging the detrimental effects of my addiction was a pivotal moment in my journey towards recovery. It allowed me to confront the underlying issues that drove me to seek solace and escape in gaming. It was a humbling realization that my addiction had been a barrier preventing me from fully engaging with and enjoying the other aspects of life that brought me joy.

Throughout my journey, I experienced several periods of abstaining from playing video games. However, the allure of gaming always managed to draw me back in, seducing me with the unique and exhilarating experiences it offered. Whether it was the heart-pounding thrill of executing a flawless aerial pinch in Rocket League alongside my best friend or the sense of camaraderie that blossomed during cooperative gameplay, these moments held an indescribable magic that seemed impossible to replicate in any other realm.

It's crucial to emphasize that the fact I could stop playing games temporarily did not diminish the intensity of my cravings or the incessant desire to immerse myself in virtual worlds. Even during those periods of abstinence, my thoughts would often drift back to the virtual battles, quests, and triumphs that awaited me. The siren song of gaming tugged at my heart, tempting me with its promises of excitement and fulfillment.

The longing for that unique sense of accomplishment and connection I experienced while gaming was powerful. It was like an itch that begged to be scratched, a hunger that demanded to be satisfied. The temporary respite from gaming only served to intensify these cravings, fueling a sense of anticipation and nostalgia for those unforgettable gaming moments.

The quest for good mental health is an intricate and multifaceted journey, one that requires introspection, self-care, and a mindful approach to life. Yet, I couldn't help but wonder how one could truly achieve a state of well-being when consumed by an all-consuming obsession, when the very essence of existence seemed to revolve around a single pursuit. In my own experiences, I struggled to find a way to strike a balance between my passions and the fundamental aspects of a fulfilling life.

How could I possibly cultivate a healthy mindset when I neglected to take care of myself? The simple pleasures that once brought me joy, like basking in the warm hues of a breathtaking sunset or cherishing the presence of loved ones, faded into the background as my obsession took precedence. Time slipped away, and the moments that could have nurtured my well-being were overshadowed by the relentless grip of my fixation.

While I may not have found all the answers, I have come to recognize the importance of balance, self-care, and introspection in nurturing my mental health. The journey towards equilibrium continues, as I navigate the complexities of life, learning to find fulfillment not only in my passions but also in the precious moments of connection, self-care, and appreciation that enrich my existence.

So, as I ponder the question of whether it is possible to achieve good mental health when consumed by an all-consuming obsession, I acknowledge that the answer may not be straightforward. It requires a delicate dance between pursuing our passions and tending to the broader aspects of well-being. It necessitates an ongoing commitment to self-awareness and a willingness to adapt and evolve. And ultimately, it is a deeply personal quest that each of us

These days, as I embark on a new chapter of my life, I have discovered the beauty in simplicity and the joy of embracing the present moment. The hurried pace and relentless obsession that once consumed my days have given way to a more balanced and fulfilling existence. Each morning, I now awaken with a sense of purpose and intention.

I have come to cherish the act of writing, dedicating a precious 15 minutes to put my thoughts and emotions onto paper. It serves as a cathartic release, a channel through which I can explore my innermost thoughts and dreams. As the words flow effortlessly from my pen, I feel a profound sense of clarity and self-expression.

After my writing ritual, I take a moment to connect with my faithful companion, my beloved dog. With a wagging tail and eyes full of adoration, she reminds me of the purest form of love and companionship. We engage in a playful exchange, a brief but meaningful connection that sets the tone for the day ahead.

Next, I make it a priority to engage in heartfelt conversations with my family. These interactions, once overshadowed by the relentless pull of my obsession, now take center stage. I listen attentively to their stories, share laughter, and offer support. It is in these moments of genuine connection that I realize the true value of human relationships, and I am grateful for the opportunity to nurture them.

As the day progresses, I carve out time to indulge in a simple pleasure that brings me immense satisfaction: preparing a delicious and nourishing meal. In the kitchen, I let my creativity roam free as I chop, stir, and season with care. The aroma of fresh ingredients fills the air, and I savor each moment, reveling in the joy of creating something nourishing for both my body and soul.

What strikes me the most about this newfound approach to my daily routine is the absence of that constant feeling of hurry and pressure. I no longer view these actions as mere tasks to be completed, but rather as invaluable moments that infuse my life with wonder and fulfillment. It is in the act of slowing down, of savoring each experience, that I have unlocked a deeper appreciation for the simple joys that surround me.

Gone are the days when I would rush through life, my mind preoccupied with the next game or virtual conquest. Instead, I have learned to cultivate a sense of presence and gratitude, embracing the beauty of the here and now. Each small act, from writing to playing with my dog, from connecting with family to preparing a meal, is a thread woven into the tapestry of my daily existence.

Through this transformation, I have discovered that the essence of a wonderful day lies not in the pursuit of external validation or in the intensity of a virtual world, but in the genuine connections I forge and the moments of self-care and appreciation I allow myself. It is in the simplicity of these actions that I find true fulfillment and a sense of purpose.

So, as I reflect upon the contrast between my past and present, I am grateful for the journey that led me to this place of balance and contentment. I now understand that true worth lies not in the speed at which I move through life, but in the depth of my experiences and the richness of my connections. And with each passing day, I embrace the wonder that unfolds in the quiet moments, discovering that the true magic of life resides in the simplicity of being fully present and cherishing every precious moment.

Chapter 3:
The Benefits of Digital Minimalism

The concept of digital minimalism and how it can be applied to combat gaming addiction

Indeed, we find ourselves immersed in a digital era, where technological devices have become an integral part of our daily lives. Phones, computers, and the vast realm of the internet have woven themselves into the fabric of our existence, permeating our routines, relationships, and even our sense of self. It is undeniable that these digital wonders offer us immense convenience, connectivity, and a world of knowledge at our fingertips.

However, amidst the allure and benefits of this interconnected world, it is easy to feel overwhelmed, consumed by a constant influx of information, notifications, and virtual demands. It is precisely in this context that we must tread the delicate path of finding balance, rather than attempting to completely sever our ties to the digital realm.

Unplugging entirely from the internet may seem like a tempting solution, a way to reclaim a sense of tranquility and simplicity. Yet, it is essential to recognize that the answer lies not in absolute disconnection, but rather in a mindful and intentional approach to our digital interactions. It is about discerning the boundary between utility and excess, between nourishment and depletion.

In our quest for a more harmonious existence, we must acknowledge that our lives are already brimming with complexities. From the multifaceted relationships we nurture, to the responsibilities we juggle, to the ambitions and aspirations that drive us forward, our days are filled with an intricate tapestry of experiences. Therefore, it is crucial not to burden ourselves further by unnecessarily overcomplicating matters.

Striving for simplicity does not entail an outright rejection of the digital world, but rather a thoughtful evaluation of its role in our lives. It involves cultivating a mindful awareness of our digital habits and their impact on our well-being. By consciously selecting the ways in which we engage with technology, we can carve out moments of respite, foster deeper connections, and navigate the complexities of modern existence with greater ease.

In this digital age, the allure of social media platforms and online content can be both enticing and overwhelming. Facebook, Instagram, TikTok, and YouTube have become synonymous with endless scrolling, mindless consumption, and a sense of detachment from the present moment. It is disheartening to recognize how easily we can get sucked into these digital realms, losing ourselves for hours at a time, only to emerge feeling unfulfilled and disconnected.

The dissatisfaction that arises from indulging in these platforms stems from the realization that they often fail to offer us anything truly valuable or meaningful. The fleeting gratification of likes, views, and viral trends can leave us craving more, perpetuating a cycle of seeking external validation and comparison. We become caught in the never-ending quest for more followers, more engagement, more digital recognition, all while sacrificing our own well-being and sense of self.

However, it is essential to acknowledge that social media and online distractions extend far beyond the realm of these popular applications. The digital landscape is vast and ever-expanding, encompassing a myriad of platforms, websites, and content that can consume our time and attention. Whether it is mindlessly browsing news articles, getting lost in a rabbit hole of online forums, or succumbing to the temptation of online shopping, there are countless ways in which we can find ourselves caught in the grip of digital distractions.

The pervasiveness of these distractions can be disconcerting, making us question the impact they have on our lives. We may wonder if the time spent engaging with these platforms and online activities is truly worth it, or if it simply adds to the noise and clutter that already permeates our existence. It is natural to feel a sense of frustration and dissatisfaction when we realize that these distractions hinder our ability to fully engage with the world around us, pursue our passions, or cultivate deep and meaningful connections with others.

To break free from the grip of digital distractions, it is important to cultivate a sense of intentionality and mindfulness in our online interactions. This starts with a conscious evaluation of the value these platforms and activities bring to our lives. We can ask ourselves if the time spent on social media or other digital distractions aligns with our values, goals, and overall well-being.

Moreover, it is crucial to create boundaries and establish healthy digital habits. This may involve setting limits on screen time, implementing designated periods of digital detox, or unfollowing accounts that no longer serve our best interests. By taking control of our digital consumption, we reclaim our time, energy, and focus, allowing us to direct them towards pursuits that truly enrich our lives.

In this process, it is important to recognize that not all digital engagement is inherently negative or detrimental. There are numerous online resources, communities, and platforms that can offer opportunities for learning, connection, and personal growth. It is about cultivating discernment and consciously curating our online experiences to align with our values and interests.

In my quest to find valuable and informative content amidst the digital noise, I discovered that there are numerous apps and platforms that offer a wealth of knowledge and insights. While I still recognize the importance of utility apps like phone, text messaging, and mobile banking, I have made a conscious decision to shift my focus away from mindless entertainment and towards sources that truly enrich my mind and broaden my horizons.

One of the most notable changes in my digital habits has been the transformation of my relationship with TikTok. Previously, whenever I opened the app, I couldn't help but feel a sense of disappointment. The endless stream of short, viral videos seemed to offer little substance or value. However, things have changed for the better.

By curating my TikTok feed and intentionally seeking out content creators who share informative and educational videos, I have been able to transform my TikTok experience into a source of inspiration and intellectual stimulation. I now come across a plethora of captivating videos that delve into various fields of knowledge, from science and history to art and philosophy.

Rather than mindlessly scrolling through an endless stream of trivial content, I find myself engaged and intrigued by the informative videos that populate my feed. These short bursts of knowledge not only pique my curiosity but also provide me with valuable insights and perspectives that I can apply to my daily life. It is truly refreshing to witness the immense potential of social media platforms when utilized in a purposeful and meaningful way.

Beyond TikTok, I have also sought out other digital resources that offer informative and thought-provoking content. Online platforms such as Medium, TED Talks, educational YouTube channels, and reputable news outlets have become my go-to sources for expanding my understanding of the world. Through engaging articles, thought-provoking essays, and enlightening videos, I have discovered a wealth of knowledge and diverse perspectives that continually challenge and enrich my thinking.

By redirecting my attention to these informative and knowledgeable platforms, I have created a digital environment that aligns more closely with my values and interests. Instead of wasting countless hours on mindless scrolling, I now spend my time engaging with content that fuels my intellectual curiosity and empowers me to learn and grow.

However, I also acknowledge the importance of maintaining a balanced approach to digital consumption. Even with the intention of seeking informative content, it is crucial to be mindful of the time spent online and ensure that it does not overshadow other aspects of life. Setting boundaries, scheduling designated periods of digital detox, and actively engaging in offline activities are essential for maintaining a well-rounded and fulfilling lifestyle.

Explore the benefits of simplifying one's digital life

Since making a conscious effort to change my habits and eliminate unnecessary distractions from my life, I have experienced a profound shift in my ability to focus on what truly matters to me. By creating a space free from digital noise and external pressures, I have opened up a realm of inner clarity and self-awareness that allows me to fully immerse myself in the present moment.

In the past, my attention was constantly divided and scattered among numerous distractions, preventing me from truly connecting with myself and appreciating the beauty of the present. However, by removing the excess noise and embracing a more intentional approach to life, I have discovered the joy of being fully present and in touch with my own desires, passions, and inner voice.

One of the most transformative aspects of this journey has been the cultivation of mindfulness. By consciously observing my thoughts, emotions, and sensations without judgment or attachment, I have developed a deeper understanding of myself and gained a heightened sense of self-awareness. This newfound clarity has allowed me to identify my true aspirations, values, and interests, and has given me the courage to pursue them wholeheartedly.

Furthermore, by simplifying my digital habits and creating more space in my life, I have been able to engage in deep thinking and introspection. With the newfound time on my hands, I have embraced the opportunity to contemplate my situation and delve into the depths of my inner world. Through this process, a crucial realization has dawned upon me: it is simply impossible to cultivate and maintain good mental health when my life revolves around an insatiable need for video games.

In the past, my fixation on video games consumed a significant portion of my time, attention, and emotional energy. Every waking moment seemed to be dedicated to seeking the next gaming experience, leaving little room for self-reflection, personal growth, and nurturing my mental well-being. It became apparent that this unbalanced focus was taking a toll on my overall happiness and fulfillment.

Through introspection, I have come to recognize that true mental health encompasses a holistic approach to well-being. It is not solely dependent on external sources of entertainment or distractions. Rather, it is rooted in a deep understanding and acceptance of oneself, as well as the cultivation of a healthy balance between various aspects of life.

Upon reflection, I came to a profound realization about a recurring theme in my struggles. It became apparent that I had been constantly seeking an activity or experience that could match the captivating and all-encompassing nature of gaming. Deep down, I yearned for something that would ignite the same sense of wonder, thrill, and fulfillment. However, I soon recognized the simple truth that if I were to discover another passion or interest that captivated me to the same extent, I would inevitably fall into the same cycle of obsession and imbalance.

This revelation led me to question the underlying reasons behind my perpetual quest for an all-consuming activity. Was it a genuine desire to explore diverse passions and engage in enriching experiences? Or was it an unconscious attempt to fill a void within myself, seeking external validation and escapism from the challenges and complexities of life?

As I delved into this introspective journey, I began to understand that true contentment and fulfillment do not lie in the pursuit of a single activity that can provide endless magic and captivation. It became clear that a sustainable and balanced approach to life involves embracing a multitude of interests, passions, and experiences that collectively contribute to a well-rounded and fulfilling existence.

Despite the lingering urges to immerse myself in gaming, the allure of those special moments where everything falls into place with perfect execution, or the comforting sense of belonging within the vast expanses of my hardcore Minecraft world, I have come to a profound realization. I now understand that while those experiences may offer fleeting excitement and temporary gratification, they pale in comparison to the deep sense of fulfillment I find in other meaningful pursuits.

Nowadays, when the temptation to indulge in gaming arises, I remind myself of the greater joys that await me when I resist those urges. Instead of succumbing to the allure of virtual adventures, I choose to channel my energy and time towards activities that bring genuine fulfillment and create lasting memories.

One such pursuit is the art of writing. I have discovered the immense satisfaction that arises from crafting my thoughts and emotions into words, whether it be through creative storytelling, personal reflection, or even engaging in thoughtful discussions. Through writing, I can explore the depths of my imagination, express my innermost thoughts, and connect with others on a profound level. The act of putting pen to paper or typing away at the keyboard allows me to express myself authentically and make sense of the world around me.

Furthermore, I have realized the immeasurable value of investing time and effort in nurturing the relationships that matter most to me. Prioritizing my family and girlfriend has become an essential part of my daily routine. I have come to cherish the moments shared with them, whether it's engaging in heartfelt conversations, offering a listening ear, or simply spending quality time together. The smiles on their faces and the warmth that radiates from those connections bring me a level of joy and contentment that no virtual world could ever replicate.

Additionally, I have discovered the joy of cooking and creating meals for my loved ones. The act of preparing a delicious dish not only nourishes their bodies but also demonstrates my love and care in a tangible way. Witnessing their enjoyment and appreciation fills me with a profound sense of fulfillment, knowing that I have contributed to their well-being and happiness through a simple act of culinary creativity.

In embracing these alternative pursuits, I have come to understand that true fulfillment and happiness lie in the richness of real-life experiences and human connections. While the allure of gaming may still linger, I recognize that the rewards of investing my time and energy in writing, nurturing relationships, and engaging in meaningful activities far outweigh the temporary thrills of virtual achievements.

Ultimately, the choice to prioritize these fulfilling endeavors requires discipline and conscious decision-making. It is a constant reminder to myself that, although gaming may provide fleeting moments of excitement and escapism, the lasting fulfillment and profound sense of purpose lie in the tangible experiences and meaningful connections that enrich my life.

Chapter 4: The Process of Change

The process of change and how to make meaningful progress towards recovery

I am still on this journey of recovery, and I have come to accept that it is a lifelong process rather than a finite destination. Each day brings its own set of challenges, but I have started to notice a gradual easing of the difficulties I initially faced. In the early stages, particularly during the first two weeks (day 0 to day 14), I encountered some of the most formidable hurdles.

It is important to grasp the extent to which gaming had ingrained itself into the fabric of my existence. For as long as I can remember, it had been my default escape, my go-to activity whenever I had completed my responsibilities or found myself with a moment of free time. The connection between finishing tasks and my mind automatically gravitating towards games was deeply rooted within me.

Breaking free from this ingrained pattern was not a simple task. It required immense self-awareness, discipline, and a willingness to confront the underlying reasons why gaming had become such a dominant force in my life. As I embarked on my recovery journey, the initial days presented a formidable test of my resolve. The void left by the absence of gaming was palpable, and I had to confront the uncomfortable reality that I had relied on this digital world to fill the gaps in my time and emotions.

During this crucial period, it was essential for me to implement new strategies and coping mechanisms. I had to redirect my focus and find alternative activities that could engage my mind and provide a sense of fulfillment. It was not an easy process, as the temptation to revert to old habits and seek solace in gaming was ever-present.

Indeed, the influence of gaming extends beyond the confines of my mind. It has permeated various aspects of my life, including my relationships, digital content consumption, and physical surroundings. The presence of gaming has been deeply intertwined with my social connections, entertainment preferences, and even the physical environment I inhabit.

For years, my friends and I have maintained our bond through gaming. Whether it was teaming up for cooperative adventures or engaging in fierce competitions, gaming provided a shared platform for us to connect and interact. It was a source of camaraderie and shared experiences, a virtual space where we could come together and enjoy each other's company. The thought of distancing myself from gaming also meant potentially altering or losing these cherished connections.

Moreover, my digital ecosystem had become saturated with gaming-related content. My YouTube feed was dominated by gameplay videos, walkthroughs, and esports competitions. It had become a habitual routine to immerse myself in this virtual world, eagerly consuming the latest updates, strategies, and discussions. The allure of gaming content was difficult to resist, often leading me down a rabbit hole of endless entertainment and distraction.

The physical artifacts of gaming further reinforced its presence in my life. My computer, a powerful vessel for virtual adventures, was adorned with countless games, ready to transport me to alternate realities at a moment's notice. The controller resting on my desk served as a constant reminder of the familiar comfort and excitement that gaming provided. Even the wallpaper on my screen depicted scenes from beloved games, serving as a visual testament to my passion.

These tangible reminders and environmental cues served as constant invitations to indulge in the world of gaming. They whispered temptations, reminding me of the excitement, escape, and gratification that awaited me with just a few clicks. Breaking free from the grasp of gaming addiction meant confronting not only the mental and emotional aspects but also the physical triggers that perpetuated the cycle.

After much contemplation and self-reflection, I made the courageous decision to go cold turkey and abruptly cease my gaming habits. It was a definitive choice, driven by a sincere desire to break free from the grip that gaming had on my life. However, I understand that the path to recovery is not a one-size-fits-all approach, and what works for one person may not necessarily work for another.

Choosing to quit gaming altogether was a deeply personal decision, one that required me to confront the extent of my addiction and acknowledge the negative impact it had on various aspects of my life. I recognized that allowing myself to play occasionally might have hindered my progress and perpetuated the cycle of addiction. For me, it was necessary to establish clear boundaries and remove gaming entirely from my daily routine.

In making this choice, I had to be honest with myself and consider what was truly best for my well-being. It was a challenging process that demanded self-discipline, resilience, and the unwavering commitment to my own recovery.

After reaching the milestone of 45 days without gaming, I cautiously entertained the idea of giving it another try. With a newfound understanding that it wasn't games themselves that were inherently bad, but rather my unhealthy obsession with them, I wanted to explore whether I could establish a healthier relationship with gaming.

Approaching this experiment with a mix of curiosity and trepidation, I set aside a specific time for gaming, allocating a strict one-hour limit. I wanted to gauge whether my perspective had shifted and if I could engage with games in a more balanced and controlled manner.

As I launched the game and immersed myself in its virtual world, I couldn't help but notice that something had changed within me. The familiar excitement and sense of escapism that used to envelop me seemed somewhat subdued. The gameplay itself was enjoyable, and I had moments of amusement and entertainment, but the experience lacked the same intensity and allure it once held.

During that hour, I found myself more aware of the passing time and the other aspects of my life that I had been neglecting. I was acutely conscious of the need to maintain a healthy balance and not allow gaming to consume my entire existence. It became evident that my priorities had shifted, and my desire for personal growth, meaningful connections, and fulfilling experiences outweighed the temporary pleasures of gaming.

Upon reflecting on my brief return to gaming, I realized that my transformation extended beyond a mere break from the activity. It was a profound shift in mindset and a reevaluation of my values and aspirations. The grip that gaming once had on me had loosened, allowing space for other pursuits that brought me greater fulfillment and personal satisfaction.

It was a perplexing paradox. On one hand, I was determined to improve myself, to embark on a journey of personal growth and well-being. Yet, on the other hand, I found myself undermining those very aspirations by engaging in behaviors that contradicted my goals. It felt akin to going for a run to enhance my physical health and then rewarding myself with a bag of candy afterward. Something felt off, out of alignment with the path I had set for myself.

While I didn't regret giving gaming another chance, it became clear that my relationship with games had fundamentally changed. What was once an all-encompassing passion now held a more modest place in my life. It no longer served as a means of escape or a primary source of entertainment but rather as an occasional recreational activity.

The experience reaffirmed my belief that moderation and self-awareness are key in navigating the world of gaming. I recognized the importance of setting boundaries and being mindful of the time and energy I invest in this digital realm. It was a reminder that balance and self-control are essential components of a healthy relationship with any form of entertainment.

It's crucial for me to reiterate that these words reflect my own experiences and perspectives. While I hope that my story resonates with some of you and provides some solace, I understand that each person's journey is unique. What worked for me may not necessarily be the solution for someone else. Therefore, if there's one key takeaway from my narrative, whether it pertains to video game addiction or any other challenge, it is this: listen to yourself.

Amidst the cacophony of external influences and conflicting desires, it is essential to tune in to your own inner voice —the voice that speaks from the depths of your being, beyond the superficial cravings or distractions. It is the voice that knows what truly brings you joy and fulfillment, the voice that guides you towards a sense of pride and self-actualization.

In a world inundated with external opinions and societal pressures, it's easy to lose sight of our own authentic desires.

Strategies for overcoming the challenges of addiction recovery

For me, one strategy that proved immensely helpful on my journey was regularly reminding myself why I made the decision to stop playing video games. I discovered that this approach is commonly recommended for individuals dealing with addiction, as it can effectively counteract the tendency to romanticize and fantasize about past experiences.

In moments of temptation or longing, it's all too easy to recall the exhilaration of those gaming sessions, the moments of triumph and camaraderie. Our minds often selectively filter out the less glamorous aspects—the frustration, the time lost, the missed opportunities, and the negative impact on our overall well-being.

By actively reminding myself of the reasons behind my choice to abstain from gaming, I brought myself back to reality. I confronted the less appealing aspects that were overshadowed by the allure of virtual adventures. I recognized the detrimental effects it had on various aspects of my life.

In my journey to overcome video game addiction, I delved into extensive research and sought understanding beyond my personal experiences. I came across numerous studies and articles discussing the concept of recidivism, typically associated with "conventional" addictions. Surprisingly, exploring this topic proved to be a valuable tool in identifying my own tendencies and potential patterns of relapse.

Recidivism, often associated with individuals returning to addictive behaviors after a period of abstinence or recovery, provided me with a framework to analyze my own journey. While video game addiction may not fit the traditional mold of substance abuse, the principles of relapse and recidivism can still apply.

By immersing myself in the literature on addiction, I gained insights into the common triggers and vulnerabilities that can lead to relapse. I learned about the importance of identifying and understanding my own personal triggers—those specific situations, emotions, or thought patterns that have historically driven me towards gaming.

Recognizing these triggers empowered me to develop proactive strategies to navigate challenging moments. I learned to anticipate potential relapse-inducing situations and implement preventative measures, such as seeking alternative activities, reaching out for support, or employing mindfulness techniques to manage cravings and urges.

Additionally, studying recidivism shed light on the significance of building a robust support network. I discovered the importance of surrounding myself with individuals who understood and supported my goals. Whether it was confiding in close friends and family or seeking guidance from support groups or therapists, having a support system proved instrumental in my recovery journey. Their understanding, encouragement, and accountability served as valuable safeguards against relapse.

Moreover, I realized that cultivating self-awareness was crucial in my efforts to break free from the cycle of addiction. Through introspection and reflection, I strived to gain a deeper understanding of my own behavioral patterns, emotional triggers, and underlying needs that gaming had temporarily fulfilled. This self-awareness enabled me to address those needs in healthier ways and develop alternative coping mechanisms.

While reading about recidivism in the context of traditional addictions, I discovered that relapses are often viewed as opportunities for growth rather than failures. This perspective resonated with me and allowed me to approach my own setbacks with compassion and a commitment to learn from them. Rather than succumbing to guilt and self-blame, I embraced relapses as valuable lessons, refining my strategies and fortifying my resilience in the face of future challenges.

It is essential to note that everyone's journey towards recovery is unique, and the principles of recidivism may manifest differently for each individual. Nevertheless, educating oneself about addiction, relapse, and recidivism can provide valuable insights and guidance along the path to recovery.

By gaining a broader perspective, understanding the experiences of others, and assimilating the knowledge from various sources, we empower ourselves with the tools necessary to navigate the complexities of addiction and reduce the likelihood of relapse. As we strive for lasting change, it is through self-reflection, education, and a willingness to adapt that we pave the way for a more fulfilling and balanced life beyond the grips of addiction.

Above all else, my unwavering determination and resolute willpower played a pivotal role in my journey to overcome video game addiction. Despite the persistent allure and intense cravings I experienced, I held steadfast to my decision to break free from the grip of gaming, never wavering in the slightest.

This unyielding resolve stemmed from the unwavering certainty I felt about my choice. I had reached a point where I recognized the detrimental impact of excessive gaming on various aspects of my life. It was no longer a matter of mere desire or fleeting motivation; it was a deeply-rooted conviction that I needed to change.

Maintaining this unshakable belief in my decision proved to be an invaluable asset throughout the recovery process. It served as a shield against doubt, self-sabotage, and the temptations that lurked around every corner. Even in moments when my longing to play became almost unbearable, I held firm to my resolve, reminding myself of the reasons why I embarked on this journey.

Chapter 5:
Finding Meaning and Purpose

The importance of finding meaning and purpose beyond gaming

Discovering alternative activities to replace gaming played a crucial role in my journey towards breaking free from the grip of addiction. It provided me with a much-needed respite from the all-consuming desire to immerse myself in the virtual world.

Initially, the void left by gaming seemed daunting. The thought of filling my time with other pursuits seemed almost unimaginable, as gaming had become an integral part of my daily routine. However, I realized that in order to reclaim my life, I needed to explore new avenues and find meaningful activities that could captivate my attention and fulfill my longing for engagement.

Embarking on my journey to find alternatives to gaming, I stumbled upon the therapeutic and rewarding world of gardening. It all began with a simple idea: creating a small garden using kitchen scraps and nurturing the seeds of various vegetables.

With a newfound enthusiasm, I gathered discarded vegetable scraps, such as carrot tops, onion bottoms, and lettuce stumps. Instead of tossing them away, I saw the potential for new life. Armed with soil, pots, and a desire to reconnect with nature, I carefully planted these scraps, eagerly anticipating their transformation into thriving plants.

To provide the seedlings with optimal conditions for growth, I invested in a full-spectrum light. Positioning it strategically above the tender sprouts, I created a nurturing environment that mimicked the warmth and radiance of natural sunlight. Each day, I attentively watered the seedlings, observing their progress and marveling at the miracle of life unfolding before my eyes.

As the days turned into weeks, my kitchen garden flourished. Vibrant green leaves unfurled, delicate stems reached for the sky, and tiny buds promised the future bounty of fresh, homegrown produce. It was a testament to the power of nurturing and patience.

As someone who had little to no experience with gardening, I embarked on a quest for knowledge to delve into the art of seed germination. Intrigued by the idea of starting my own plants from tiny seeds, I sought out resources to equip myself with the necessary skills and understanding.

Determined to make the most of my gardening venture, I delved into the world of literature, online forums, and gardening communities. My search for information on seed germination led me on a captivating journey, filled with a wealth of insights and valuable tips from seasoned gardeners.

Immersing myself in the subject, I discovered a vast array of resources that offered guidance on everything from seed selection to optimal planting conditions. The internet became my virtual classroom, providing me with a plethora of articles, videos, and step-by-step guides that illuminated the path to successful seed germination.

However, as I delved deeper into my research, I realized that while I found valuable information, I was still searching for something more. I yearned for a comprehensive guide tailored to my specific needs and desires, one that would not only provide technical knowledge but also ignite my passion and make the process truly enjoyable.

Writing a book had long been a cherished dream residing within the depths of my bucket list. Fueled by the passion and knowledge I had acquired through my journey of seed germination, I embarked on a new endeavor—to share my insights and experiences with fellow gardening enthusiasts. And so, with determination and a sense of purpose, I began to pen my creation: "Grow Your Garden: The Essential Seed Germination Handbook."

The process of transforming my thoughts, experiences, and accumulated wisdom into a cohesive and informative book was an adventure in itself. I meticulously organized the wealth of information I had gathered, ensuring that each chapter flowed seamlessly and that the content was accessible to both novice gardeners and seasoned experts alike.

As a self-professed perfectionist, I had always held myself to high standards and had a tendency to nitpick my own achievements. So, when I completed my first book, "Grow Your Garden: The Essential Seed Germination Handbook," I experienced a mix of emotions. While I may not have been entirely satisfied with every minute detail, there was an undeniable sense of happiness and accomplishment that permeated my being. I had taken the time and effort to see this project through to the end, and that in itself was a significant milestone worth celebrating.

The completion of "Grow Your Garden" not only fulfilled a long-standing item on my bucket list but also marked a turning point in my personal growth. It served as a reminder that I had the ability to overcome challenges, conquer self-doubt, and channel my energy into creative pursuits that extended beyond the realm of gaming.

Buoyed by the success of my first book, I felt inspired to continue my journey as an author and explore new avenues of expression. Drawing from my own experiences and the lessons I had learned about cultivating meaningful connections, I embarked on my second literary endeavor: "How to be Loved."

In "How to be Loved," I delved into a plethora of love-related topics, inviting readers to embark on a heartfelt exploration of human connections, self-love, and the intricacies of relationships. From understanding the importance of self-care and setting healthy boundaries to fostering empathy and cultivating deep, meaningful connections, the book aimed to provide readers with practical guidance and thought-provoking insights.

But writing wasn't my initial pursuit in my quest for something captivating. For a consecutive two weeks, I embarked on a daily exploration of various creative endeavors, hoping to stumble upon a passion that would ignite my soul. Each day was a blank canvas, eagerly awaiting the stroke of my artistic experimentation.

With an open mind and a thirst for discovery, I ventured into the realms of drawing, venturing beyond the traditional medium to explore the possibilities of digital artistry. I immersed myself in the intricacies of 3D sculpting and animation, pushing the boundaries of my imagination and skill set.

Undeterred by initial setbacks or moments of frustration, I embraced the journey of trial and error as I dabbled in the enchanting world of 2D animation. The process of breathing life into still images through movement and storytelling captivated my senses, driving me to refine my techniques and bring my ideas to fruition.

But my exploration did not end there. I eagerly delved into the realm of music creation, experimenting with melodies, harmonies, and rhythms that resonated with the depths of my being. Through the creation of melodies and the harmonization of instruments, I sought to express the emotions that words alone could not capture.

I also ventured into the realm of written expression beyond book authorship. The creation of a blog became an avenue through which I could share my thoughts, experiences, and discoveries with a wider audience. It allowed me to delve into a myriad of topics, from personal growth and creativity to the wonders of the natural world, all while honing my skills as a writer. In a burst of creativity, I explored the art of bracelet-making, weaving intricate patterns and colors together to form wearable pieces of self-expression. The act of creating something tangible, with each knot and bead representing a piece of my journey, brought a sense of satisfaction and fulfillment.

Intrigued by the captivating world of Dungeons and Dragons, I found myself immersed in the art of storytelling, crafting intricate narratives and bringing characters to life within the confines of a tabletop game. It became a collaborative outlet for creativity, where imagination and camaraderie intertwined to create unforgettable adventures.

The allure of worldbuilding beckoned, prompting me to embark on a journey of creating vibrant, immersive universes from scratch. From intricately detailed maps to the development of unique cultures and histories, I reveled in the power of imagination, sculpting entire worlds that existed solely within the realm of my mind.

To immerse myself in diverse narratives, I immersed myself in the world of manga, exploring captivating storylines and breathtaking artwork that transcended cultural boundaries. The visual storytelling and vibrant illustrations served as a wellspring of inspiration, fueling my own creative endeavors.

Not content with the visual realm alone, I delved into the enchanting melodies and heartfelt emotions of anime soundtracks. The harmonious blend of music and storytelling resonated deeply within me, transporting me to distant worlds and evoking a myriad of emotions.

As I look back on those two weeks of boundless exploration, I am amazed by the breadth and depth of the creative endeavors I pursued. While some ventures resonated more strongly than others, each experience contributed to my growth as an individual, broadening my horizons and fueling my desire to discover my true passion.

Although writing ultimately emerged as my creative sanctuary, it was the culmination of countless trials and experiences that led me to this realization. The journey of exploration allowed me to uncover hidden talents, develop new skills, and gain a deeper understanding of myself and the world around me.

And while I may not remember every single endeavor I embarked upon during those two weeks, the essence of that period remains etched in my memory—an embodiment of the unyielding spirit of curiosity and the unwavering pursuit of something captivating.

In the end, it was the diversity of my explorations that shaped me into the person I am today—a multifaceted individual with a thirst for creative expression and an insatiable curiosity for the world.

Indeed, the journey of discovering something that truly resonates with your heart and brings you a sense of pride and fulfillment is not always an easy one. It requires patience, self-reflection, and a willingness to explore different avenues until you stumble upon that elusive passion that sets your soul on fire.

The process of finding something you truly love is akin to embarking on a treasure hunt. You venture into uncharted territory, open to new experiences and possibilities.

Ways to find fulfillment and joy in non-digital activities

One of the aspects of writing books that I found particularly fulfilling was the concept of passive income. It felt like a dream come true to have the opportunity to generate income from my creativity, something I had always considered to be a personal passion rather than a potential source of financial stability.

The idea of passive income, in its essence, refers to the ability to earn money with minimal effort once the initial work has been completed. For me, this meant that even when I wasn't actively writing or promoting my books, they continued to generate income. It was a truly liberating feeling to know that my creative endeavors could have a lasting impact on my financial well-being.

Having the opportunity to earn passive income through writing allowed me to embrace a sense of freedom and flexibility in my life.

The sense of pride and fulfillment that came from building something tangible through my writing was incomparable to the virtual achievements I had experienced in gaming. In the digital realm, my gaming accomplishments had been fleeting, existing only within the confines of the game itself. They held little value beyond the virtual world, serving as mere pixels on a screen.

However, with writing, it was different. Each book I completed became a physical manifestation of my creativity and hard work. Holding a physical copy of my book in my hands filled me with a profound sense of accomplishment and pride. It was a testament to my dedication, perseverance, and the countless hours I had invested in crafting a meaningful piece of work.

Unlike gaming achievements that often lacked a real-life impact, my books had the potential to make a genuine difference in the lives of others. Through my writing, I could share knowledge, inspire, and entertain readers. The thought that my words could resonate with someone, evoke emotions, or provide valuable insights was immensely gratifying.

In my book "How to be Loved," I delve into the realm of love and relationships, exploring the magical and transformative power they hold. I share insights, advice, and personal experiences that shed light on the profound fulfillment that can be found in opening oneself up to the possibility of love.

Love, in all its forms, has an enchanting quality that transcends the virtual realm of gaming. It is a deeply human experience that touches our souls and allows us to connect with others on a profound level. While gaming may provide temporary excitement and fleeting moments of joy, the depths of love and the genuine connections it fosters offer a lasting and profound sense of fulfillment.

Embarking on the journey of finding love requires courage and vulnerability. It is an act of opening oneself up to another person, allowing them to see our true selves and embracing the possibility of rejection or heartache. But it is through this courageous leap that we give ourselves the opportunity to experience a love that can bring immeasurable joy, growth, and fulfillment.

Love encompasses a multitude of forms: romantic love, platonic love, familial love, and self-love. Each holds its own unique beauty and potential for fulfillment. Through genuine connections with others, we can experience love's transformative power. The joy of sharing life's moments, the support and understanding offered by loved ones, and the sense of belonging that comes from being truly seen and accepted create a tapestry of fulfillment that surpasses the fleeting pleasures of gaming.

Ultimately, the choice between gaming and pursuing love is a deeply personal one. However, from my own experiences and reflections, I have found that the journey of love offers a richness and fulfillment that surpasses the allure of virtual achievements. It requires courage, vulnerability, and the willingness to embrace the unknown. But the rewards, the depth of connection, and the transformative power of love make it a worthy pursuit—one that holds immeasurable worth and surpasses the transient pleasures of gaming.

In the end, the pursuit of fulfillment and personal satisfaction comes down to discovering what truly resonates with you. Reflecting on the aspects of gaming that brought you joy can serve as valuable clues in finding activities and experiences that can replicate or even surpass those feelings in real life.

Consider the games you enjoyed the most, like Minecraft. Did you find satisfaction in building a cozy home and nurturing a virtual pet dog? Perhaps the creativity and sense of accomplishment that came from constructing intricate structures with redstone mechanisms fascinated you. Or maybe it was the social aspect of gaming that captivated you, where you could connect and converse with a diverse community of friends. Alternatively, the competitive nature of gaming might have driven you to strive for excellence and push your limits.

Take these insights as starting points to explore similar avenues in the real world. If you enjoyed building in Minecraft, you might find pleasure in engaging in DIY projects or pursuing architecture or interior design. Creating tangible, aesthetically pleasing spaces that bring you comfort and joy can be incredibly fulfilling. Additionally, exploring hobbies like sculpting, painting, or writing can unleash your creative side and provide an outlet for self-expression.

If the social aspect of gaming appealed to you, seek out opportunities to connect with others in real life. Join clubs, organizations, or online communities centered around shared interests, where you can engage in meaningful conversations and build connections with like-minded individuals. Cultivating relationships and nurturing friendships outside of the virtual realm can bring a sense of belonging and support that surpasses the temporary interactions found in gaming.

For those who thrived on competition, consider exploring sports, board games, or even e-sports tournaments where you can challenge yourself and experience the adrenaline rush of healthy competition. Engaging in activities that push your limits, whether physically or mentally, can provide a sense of achievement and personal growth.

It's essential to approach this journey of self-discovery with an open mind and a willingness to explore new territories. Embrace the mindset of a gamer seeking a new game to immerse themselves in, except this time, the game is life itself. Allow yourself to experiment, try new activities, and step out of your comfort zone. It's through these explorations that you can uncover new passions, discover hidden talents, and experience a genuine sense of fulfillment.

Remember, the goal is not to replace gaming entirely but to find a balance that allows you to engage in activities that bring you lasting joy and personal satisfaction. By tapping into the elements that made gaming enjoyable for you, you can create a life that incorporates those same elements and surpasses the transient pleasures of virtual worlds.

It's important to acknowledge that games hold a special place in our lives. They provide us with immersive experiences, memorable moments, and even profound connections with others. Those memories are real and hold genuine value. However, the decision to step away from gaming is rooted in recognizing that there are reasons beyond those cherished memories that necessitated a change.

The reason that led you to take a break from gaming is valid and should be honored. It could be a multitude of factors, such as prioritizing other aspects of life, maintaining a healthy balance, or addressing addictive tendencies. Whatever the reason, it's crucial to remind yourself of it and stay committed to your chosen path.

While acknowledging the positive aspects of gaming, it's equally important to remember the reasons why you chose to step away. Perhaps gaming was consuming excessive amounts of your time and hindering your personal growth or affecting your relationships and responsibilities. By staying connected to the underlying motivation behind your decision, you can maintain clarity and reinforce your determination.

It's essential to find alternative activities and pursuits that align with your values, aspirations, and overall well-being. By redirecting your time and energy towards endeavors that bring you a sense of pride, fulfillment, and personal growth, you can create a life that encompasses a wide range of meaningful experiences beyond the virtual realm.

Chapter 6:
The Power of Connection

The importance of social connection in addiction recovery

Our social circle, both offline and online, undeniably influences our perspectives and choices in significant ways. The people we surround ourselves with can shape our thoughts, beliefs, and even our habits. This holds true for both our physical interactions with friends, family, and acquaintances, as well as our virtual connections through social media platforms and online communities.

Consider the example you mentioned earlier regarding your YouTube feed being inundated with video game-related content. It's natural that constant exposure to such content would make it challenging to distance yourself from the world of gaming. Our online environments often reinforce our existing interests and preferences by presenting us with tailored recommendations and updates based on our browsing history and engagement patterns. This can create a sort of echo chamber, where we find ourselves continuously exposed to content that aligns with our existing inclinations.

Recognizing the influence of our social circles, both offline and online, is crucial in understanding how they can impact our thoughts and behaviors. It's essential to be mindful of the content we consume, the communities we engage with, and the conversations we participate in. By consciously curating our online experiences and diversifying our sources of information and inspiration, we can broaden our perspectives and reduce the overwhelming presence of any single interest or topic.

The influence of our friends and close ones cannot be understated when it comes to shaping our choices and behaviors. Just as our online connections can impact our perspectives, the people we surround ourselves with in our daily lives hold significant sway over our actions and interests.

In your case, having a circle of friends who are all avid gamers and engaging in daily gaming sessions together created a strong bond and shared experiences. It's evident that gaming played a central role in your relationships, serving as a common ground for connection and shared enjoyment. However, as you embarked on your journey to change your gaming habits, it's natural that this shift had an impact on your friendships.

The dynamics of any relationship can be affected when one person makes a significant change in their lifestyle or interests. In this case, your decision to step away from gaming inevitably had repercussions for your relationships with your gaming friends. It's worth acknowledging that change can sometimes create a temporary strain as people adjust to new circumstances and find common ground in different activities or topics.

Indeed, it would be incredibly challenging and disheartening if your friends didn't support your decision to step away from gaming and instead insisted on you continuing to play. It takes immense courage and self-awareness to recognize that a change in behavior is necessary for your personal well-being and growth. In such a scenario, where your friends are not understanding or supportive, it can create a significant internal conflict.

When we value the opinions and acceptance of our friends, their ridicule or dismissal of our choices can be emotionally distressing. It can make us question ourselves, our motives, and even the strength of our friendships. The conflicting feelings of wanting to please our friends while also honoring our own desires and needs can be overwhelming.

In these instances, it's crucial to remember that your journey towards personal growth and self-improvement is unique to you. It's okay to have different perspectives and goals. True friends should respect your individuality, support your decisions, and celebrate your efforts to pursue what you believe is best for your own happiness and well-being.

It can be helpful to have an open and honest conversation with your friends about your decision and the reasons behind it. Clearly expressing your feelings and explaining how gaming may have affected your life can provide them with insight into your perspective. While it's understandable that they may not fully comprehend your reasons initially, open dialogue can foster empathy and understanding.

In some cases, friends who initially resist or ridicule your decision may eventually come to appreciate and respect the positive changes you're making in your life. By staying true to yourself and confidently pursuing your path, you might inspire them to reflect on their own behaviors and choices. Sometimes, it takes time for others to adjust to and understand personal transformations, and patience can be crucial in such situations.

However, it's essential to remember that you deserve friends who uplift and support you. If your friends continue to push you to engage in activities that are not aligned with your goals or belittle your choices, it might be necessary to evaluate the healthiness of those friendships. Surrounding yourself with individuals who respect and encourage your personal growth is vital for your own well-being and happiness.

Amidst the challenges of shifting away from gaming and the potential strain it can place on friendships, it is crucial to recognize and appreciate the true friends who stand by you and support your journey. While it may seem like these individuals are few and far between, the value they bring to your life is immeasurable. If you are fortunate enough to have even one genuine and supportive friend, it is essential to cherish that connection and allow it to guide you through your recovery process.

True friends are those who genuinely care about your well-being and have your best interests at heart. They are the ones who listen without judgment, offer a helping hand, and provide a source of comfort and encouragement during challenging times. These friends may not fully understand your struggle with gaming addiction, but they acknowledge your journey and respect your decision to make positive changes in your life.

In times of vulnerability and transition, having someone who stands by your side can make all the difference. They serve as a pillar of strength, offering unwavering support and understanding when you need it the most. Whether it's lending a listening ear, providing words of wisdom, or engaging in activities that align with your newfound interests, these friends become invaluable allies in your recovery process.

Building and nurturing these genuine connections can provide a sense of belonging and a safe space to share your thoughts, concerns, and triumphs.

I discovered that one effective strategy to overcome the urges and challenges associated with gaming addiction was to engage in open and honest conversations with someone I trust. By sharing my thoughts and feelings with another person, I found immense relief and support that significantly aided me in navigating through difficult moments.

Voicing our inner struggles and thoughts can have a profound impact on our emotional well-being. It provides an opportunity to release pent-up emotions, gain clarity, and receive valuable feedback and perspective from a compassionate listener. Talking it out with someone allows us to externalize our thoughts, making them less overwhelming and more manageable.

When we openly discuss our gaming urges and the temptations we face, we shed light on the underlying triggers and motivations behind our addictive behavior. This process of self-reflection, coupled with the empathetic support of a trusted individual, helps us gain a deeper understanding of ourselves and our addiction. It enables us to identify patterns, uncover root causes, and develop effective coping strategies.

Strategies for building supportive relationships and finding community

Constructing a supportive friend group or community can indeed be a daunting task, especially for individuals who identify as shy introverts like myself. The prospect of opening up and seeking support may seem intimidating at first, but it's important to remember that everyone's journey is unique and that there are various avenues for finding understanding and compassionate listeners.

For those who struggle with forming connections outside their immediate circle, turning to close family members can be a valuable starting point. Siblings, parents, or even that one aunt who has always shown unwavering support can offer a safe space to share your thoughts and emotions. These familial bonds often come with a sense of trust and familiarity that can alleviate the initial anxiety of opening up.

Engaging in conversations with family members can be particularly beneficial due to the existing level of closeness and shared history. They may have witnessed your gaming habits firsthand and can provide a compassionate perspective, free from judgment or misunderstandings. Additionally, family members often have a vested interest in your well-being and are motivated to support your journey towards recovery.

If, however, familial connections are not readily available or conducive to open discussions about gaming addiction, consider exploring other avenues for support. This could involve reaching out to trusted friends or acquaintances who have demonstrated understanding and empathy in the past. Sometimes, individuals within our social circles surprise us with their willingness to listen and offer support when given the opportunity.

Moreover, it's important to acknowledge that speaking with someone about your struggles does not necessarily require forming a large social circle. Even just one supportive and trustworthy individual can make a significant difference in your recovery journey. Their presence and willingness to listen can provide a much-needed outlet for expressing your thoughts, fears, and aspirations.

For shy introverts, the thought of initiating conversations may feel overwhelming. However, remember that vulnerability and courage often go hand in hand. Taking that first step and opening up about your experiences with gaming addiction can create a sense of relief and pave the way for deeper connections.

If face-to-face conversations feel too intimidating, alternative methods of communication can also be explored. Writing a heartfelt letter or sending a thoughtful message can provide an opportunity to express yourself at your own pace, allowing you to articulate your thoughts more effectively.

In addition to personal connections, there are online communities and support groups specifically tailored to individuals dealing with gaming addiction. These communities offer a platform where you can connect with like-minded individuals who understand the challenges you face. Participating in online discussions or attending virtual support group meetings can provide a sense of camaraderie and encouragement, even for introverts who may find solace in the anonymity of the online space.

Turning to online platforms such as Reddit and other forums can indeed be an excellent starting point for seeking support when there are limited options within your immediate social circle. The beauty of these online communities lies in their ability to bring together individuals who share similar experiences and challenges. In the context of gaming addiction, engaging with like-minded individuals in these forums can offer a unique sense of understanding and empathy that may be harder to find in other settings.

When searching for support, it's crucial to find a community that aligns with your specific needs. Navigating through forums dedicated to gaming addiction or related topics can provide valuable insights, firsthand experiences, and practical advice from individuals who have faced similar struggles. Engaging with these communities not only allows you to share your own story but also provides an opportunity to learn from the experiences of others, gain new perspectives, and discover coping mechanisms that have proven successful for different individuals.

One of the most valuable lessons I've learned from my interactions is the power of honesty and openness about my struggles. This approach has allowed me to cultivate relationships that are primarily positive, and I attribute this to two main reasons. Firstly, by being transparent about my challenges, I can quickly identify individuals whose attitudes or behaviors may have a negative impact on my well-being. While it can make certain interactions more difficult, I firmly believe that the benefits outweigh the drawbacks. Being upfront about my struggles allows me to see through pretense and form genuine connections with people who accept and support me for who I am.

Secondly, when we open up about our own challenges, we create an environment where others feel comfortable sharing their own struggles. By demonstrating vulnerability, we establish a sense of trust and understanding that encourages honest communication. This can be particularly beneficial when interacting with individuals who are also going through their own difficulties. Knowing that someone else can relate to their experiences or at least provide a non-judgmental ear can be incredibly comforting and empowering. It fosters a sense of camaraderie and mutual support, where both parties can lend a listening ear and offer empathy without fear of judgment.

Being honest and open about our struggles also helps to break down barriers and reduce the stigma surrounding mental health and personal challenges. By engaging in authentic conversations, we contribute to a culture of acceptance and understanding. This creates an environment where people feel safe to seek support and express their true selves without fear of rejection or discrimination.

Of course, it's important to exercise discernment in sharing personal struggles. Not everyone deserves or is equipped to handle our vulnerabilities, so it's crucial to choose trustworthy individuals with whom to open up. Seek out those who have demonstrated empathy, understanding, and the capacity for active listening.

Discussing addiction or any personal problem is undoubtedly challenging. It requires immense courage and vulnerability to confront our struggles and acknowledge them, both to ourselves and to others. I can empathize with the difficulty of this process, as I, too, have faced moments of resistance and internal struggle when addressing my own addictive tendencies.

As someone who values objectivity, honesty, and making decisions that are in my best interest, accepting the suggestion to stop playing video games was initially a bitter pill to swallow. Even though I had independently arrived at the realization that my gaming habits were becoming detrimental, it was still difficult to fully embrace the notion that quitting would significantly benefit me. Admitting this to myself was a humbling experience, as it required confronting my own vulnerabilities and acknowledging the potential negative impact of my gaming addiction.

Furthermore, when my parents also recognized the need for me to cut back on gaming, it stirred up a mix of emotions. On one hand, their agreement with my self-assessment provided validation that I wasn't alone in recognizing the issue. On the other hand, it was challenging to accept their support and advice, as part of me resisted any external influence, even if it was well-intentioned and came from a place of love.

The reason I'm sharing my personal experience with you all is to emphasize that even in the most favorable situations, we may encounter words that hurt us. Our loved ones, although well-meaning, might not always possess the most effective communication techniques. It's crucial to understand that, in most cases, their intentions are rooted in genuine care and concern for our well-being. While their delivery may be flawed, it's essential to take a moment to breathe and reflect on the underlying intent behind their message.

During difficult conversations, it's natural to feel a range of emotions, including hurt, frustration, or defensiveness. However, it's important to separate the impact of their words from the intention behind them. Remind yourself that the intent of their message was likely not to cause harm but rather to express their perspective, share their observations, or offer guidance based on their genuine concern for your welfare.

In such moments, taking a step back to gain perspective can be immensely beneficial. Give yourself the space to process your emotions and understand that their words might be a result of their own limitations in expressing their thoughts effectively. It's essential to remember that no one is perfect when it comes to communication, and even those closest to us can stumble in conveying their concerns or advice.

By pausing and reflecting on their intentions, you can prevent misunderstandings and foster a more constructive dialogue. Try to see beyond the delivery and focus on the core message they are trying to convey. Look for the underlying care, love, and genuine desire to help you overcome your challenges.

Additionally, open and honest communication can play a pivotal role in such situations. Express your feelings, concerns, or uncertainties to your loved ones, sharing how their words impacted you. This allows for a deeper understanding of one another's perspectives and encourages a more supportive and empathetic exchange moving forward.

Chapter 7: Mindfulness and Self-Care

The role of mindfulness and self-care in addiction recovery

In all aspects of life, including recovery, mindfulness and self-care play crucial roles. Mindfulness, for those who may not be familiar, is the practice of intentionally directing our attention and awareness to the present moment, without judgment or attachment. It involves observing our thoughts, emotions, and bodily sensations with a non-reactive and accepting attitude.

In the context of recovery, mindfulness can be an invaluable tool. It allows us to become more aware of our cravings, triggers, and emotional states without automatically giving in to them. By cultivating mindfulness, we develop the ability to pause and observe our inner experiences without immediately reacting or succumbing to impulsive behaviors. This heightened awareness enables us to make conscious choices aligned with our recovery goals, rather than being driven solely by urges or old patterns.

Moreover, self-care is an essential component of the recovery journey. Self-care encompasses a range of activities and practices that individuals engage in to nurture their physical, mental, and emotional well-being. It involves recognizing our personal needs and deliberately prioritizing activities that promote joy, relaxation, and rejuvenation.

Engaging in self-care is not selfish; it is an act of self-preservation and self-compassion. It allows us to replenish our energy reserves, reduce stress, and enhance our overall well-being. Self-care practices can vary greatly from person to person, as each individual has unique preferences and needs. It could involve activities such as engaging in hobbies, spending time in nature, practicing relaxation techniques, engaging in physical exercise, seeking therapy or counseling, connecting with loved ones, setting boundaries, and practicing self-compassion.

By incorporating mindfulness and self-care into our recovery journey, we develop a stronger foundation for sustainable change. Mindfulness helps us cultivate a deeper understanding of ourselves and our experiences, empowering us to make conscious choices that align with our values and goals. Self-care nurtures our overall well-being, fostering resilience, self-compassion, and a sense of balance in our lives.

In your journey to recovery, it's natural to experience urges and temptations to revert back to your gaming habits. Gaming may have become deeply ingrained in your routine, and it's where you have created numerous positive memories. Additionally, it can be tempting to choose the familiar path rather than venturing into the unknown territory of personal growth and self-improvement.

One of the primary reasons it's challenging to break free from gaming is because it has become a habit. Our brains are wired to seek out familiar patterns and engage in activities that provide instant gratification. Gaming often offers a sense of excitement, achievement, and escapism, making it difficult to let go of the comfort it provides. Breaking free from a habit requires conscious effort, self-awareness, and the development of alternative coping mechanisms.

Furthermore, the emotional attachment to gaming can be powerful. It's not just the gameplay itself but the memories associated with it—laughing with friends, overcoming challenges, and experiencing moments of triumph. These positive associations can trigger a sense of longing and nostalgia, making it tempting to return to gaming as a means of reliving those cherished memories. However, it's important to recognize that true growth and fulfillment come from exploring new avenues and embracing personal development.

But it's crucial to avoid being harsh on yourself during this process. Experiencing urges and even succumbing to your addiction does not define you as a failure or reflect negatively on your character. It simply signifies that you are human and in need of support and assistance.

Recovering from addiction is a complex journey, and setbacks are a common part of the process. It's important to approach these setbacks with understanding, compassion, and a willingness to seek help. Remember, addiction is not a personal flaw or a sign of weakness, but rather a challenge that requires guidance and support to overcome. Instead of berating yourself for giving in to urges, try to view it as an opportunity for self-reflection and growth. Explore the triggers that led to the relapse and identify strategies to manage them effectively in the future. Recognize that recovery is a continuous learning process, and setbacks can provide valuable insights and lessons along the way.

Seeking help is not a sign of weakness, but an act of strength and self-awareness. Reach out to supportive individuals in your life, such as friends, family members, or professionals who specialize in addiction recovery. They can offer guidance, encouragement, and resources to help you navigate the challenges you face.

Strategies for practicing mindfulness and self-care to promote wellbeing
And I am here to offer my assistance in your journey towards recovery. One powerful tool that can aid you in distancing yourself from the urges and obsessions is the practice of mindfulness. By incorporating mindfulness into your daily life, you can cultivate a greater sense of self-awareness, develop the ability to observe your thoughts and emotions without judgment, and create space between yourself and the impulses that arise.

Mindfulness involves bringing your attention to the present moment and fully experiencing it without getting caught up in thoughts of the past or worries about the future. It encourages you to pay attention to the sensations in your body, the thoughts passing through your mind, and the emotions that arise, all with a non-reactive and accepting attitude. This practice allows you to observe your urges and cravings without automatically giving in to them, as you develop a deeper understanding of their transient nature.

When you notice an urge or obsession arising, rather than allowing it to consume you, take a moment to pause and acknowledge its presence. Allow yourself to fully experience the sensations and thoughts associated with it, without judgment or resistance. By bringing your attention to the present moment, you can detach yourself from the grip of the urge and gain clarity on whether or not acting upon it aligns with your values and goals.

In moments when the allure of going back to gaming becomes tempting, it is essential to pause and reflect on the reality of that choice. Our minds often romanticize the positive aspects of gaming, focusing on the excitement, escapism, and sense of achievement. However, it is equally important to remember the negative consequences that can arise from indulging in this habit.

Recall the times when gaming consumed your life to the point where you neglected your responsibilities and relationships. Reflect on the moments when you chose to isolate yourself from loved ones, missing out on meaningful connections and shared experiences. Remember the feelings of regret and guilt that accompanied those times, as well as the toll it took on your mental and emotional well-being.

Think about the adverse effects gaming had on your overall lifestyle. Consider the hours and days lost in front of a screen, where time slipped away without any tangible accomplishments or personal growth. Reflect on the physical effects, such as the sedentary lifestyle that often accompanies excessive gaming, leading to decreased fitness and overall health.

Recalling these negative experiences and consequences does not mean dwelling in self-blame or punishment. Instead, it serves as a reminder of why you embarked on the path of recovery in the first place. It helps to reframe the allure of gaming by highlighting the potential harm it can cause to your well-being and the relationships that matter most to you.

When it comes to self-care, it's crucial to approach it from a holistic perspective. While gaming may provide a temporary sense of relaxation, it's worth exploring other activities that can contribute to your overall well-being.

Consider a scenario where you find yourself feeling exhausted and in need of relaxation. It may be tempting to turn to gaming as a means to unwind. However, it's worth pausing and considering alternative self-care practices that can have a more profound and lasting impact on both your mind and body.

Imagine taking the time to indulge in a warm bath, allowing the soothing water to envelop you while you let your mind wander freely. In this moment of tranquility, you give yourself the opportunity to unwind not just physically, but also mentally and emotionally. As your thoughts flow, you may find that this reflective time brings about a sense of clarity, introspection, and rejuvenation.

Engaging in activities like taking a bath, going for a walk in nature, practicing mindfulness or meditation, journaling, or engaging in a hobby that brings you joy can provide a more comprehensive form of self-care. These activities allow you to address not only your immediate need for relaxation but also nurture your overall well-being.

Self-care is not solely about finding momentary relief but also about making choices that promote long-term physical, mental, and emotional health. By exploring alternative self-care practices, you open yourself up to a range of possibilities that can truly benefit you on multiple levels.

It's important to acknowledge that for some, the idea of being alone with their thoughts can be intimidating and uncomfortable. If you find yourself feeling this way, I encourage you to reflect on the reasons behind your fear and explore how you can address it.

Consider why you perceive your thoughts as dark and why you feel the need to constantly escape from them. What are the underlying concerns or anxieties that make facing your thoughts seem daunting? It's possible that these thoughts represent unresolved emotions, past traumas, or self-doubt that you've been avoiding.

Chapter 8: Moving Forward

The ongoing process of addiction recovery and the importance of continued growth and learning

In my personal experience, addiction recovery is a lifelong journey, much like managing my mental health. At first, the idea of facing this ongoing battle may seem daunting and overwhelming. However, I've come to believe that it doesn't have to be a frightening prospect. Instead, it can be viewed as a series of small changes made over time, each contributing to the construction of a solid foundation for a brighter future.

Recovery is not a quick fix or an instant transformation. It is a gradual process of self-discovery, healing, and personal growth. Recognizing that recovery is an ongoing journey allows us to approach it with patience, self-compassion, and the understanding that setbacks may occur along the way.

By breaking down the recovery process into smaller, manageable steps, it becomes less overwhelming and more achievable. Each small change, whether it's developing healthier coping mechanisms, seeking support, or adopting positive habits, contributes to the strengthening of our foundation for long-term well-being.

I invite you to visualize the process of addiction recovery as a beaver building a dam. At first glance, a single branch or stick may seem insignificant and incapable of withstanding the force of a rushing river. However, it is through the accumulation of these small building blocks that the impossible becomes possible. In the same way, by focusing on developing one positive habit or making one constructive change at a time, you can create a powerful barrier against addiction and pave the way for a transformative recovery.

Just like a beaver methodically places each branch, twig, and stone to construct a sturdy dam, you too can approach your recovery with a step-by-step mindset. Start by identifying one area of your life that you wish to improve or one negative pattern you want to break. It could be establishing a consistent sleep schedule, incorporating regular exercise into your routine, seeking therapy or counseling, or practicing mindfulness and self-reflection. Select one aspect and commit to making small, manageable changes in that area.

Similar to how a beaver's dam gradually grows stronger with each addition, your resilience and progress will build over time as you implement positive habits and make healthier choices. Acknowledge that change takes patience and perseverance. There may be setbacks along the way, but remember that each setback is an opportunity for learning and growth. Keep the ultimate goal in sight while focusing on the present moment and the small actions you can take today.

It's important to recognize that building a dam or recovering from addiction is not a solitary endeavor. Just as beavers work together to construct their dams, seeking support from others is crucial in your journey of recovery. Connect with individuals who understand your experiences, whether it's through support groups, counseling, or online communities. Surround yourself with a network of people who can provide guidance, encouragement, and empathy.

As you continue building your dam of recovery, remember that it's not solely about preventing the "water" of addiction from flowing. It's also about redirecting that energy into healthier channels. Consider what positive experiences, activities, and relationships you can cultivate to replace the void left by addiction. Explore new hobbies, rediscover old passions, nurture meaningful connections, and engage in self-care practices that contribute to your overall well-being.

In the process of constructing your dam, you may encounter challenges, doubts, and moments of fatigue. However, hold onto the image of the determined beaver, persistently adding one stick at a time, and envision the strength and resilience you are building within yourself. Allow yourself to be inspired by the progress you have made, no matter how small, and celebrate each milestone along the way.

Remember, just as a beaver's dam can redirect the flow of a river, you have the power to redirect the course of your life. By focusing on one positive change at a time, remaining connected to supportive communities, and nurturing a mindset of perseverance, you can create a strong foundation for lasting recovery. Embrace the journey, trust in your ability to adapt and grow, and believe in the transformative power of incremental change.

Resources and support for readers seeking to continue their journey towards recovery

This is a heartfelt message for those who have embarked on the courageous journey of addiction recovery. First and foremost, I want to express my sincere congratulations to you for taking that crucial first step of acknowledging the challenges you face. It takes immense strength and self-awareness to recognize the need for change, and you have shown immense courage in doing so.

I want you to know that I wholeheartedly believe in you and your ability to overcome this obstacle. By simply reading this book and actively seeking guidance and support, you have already demonstrated a commitment to your own well-being and growth. This is a significant accomplishment in itself, and it is a testament to your resilience and determination.

Recovery is not an easy path, but you have shown that you possess the right mindset and attitude to navigate it successfully. Your willingness to learn, grow, and take action is truly inspiring. You have chosen to take responsibility for your own healing and have embraced the power of self-improvement.

As you continue on this journey, it's important to remember that setbacks and challenges may arise. Recovery is not a linear process, and there may be times when you feel discouraged or face obstacles that seem insurmountable. But in those moments, I want you to hold on to the belief that you can overcome anything you set your mind to.

Take each day as it comes and celebrate even the smallest victories along the way. Recognize and appreciate the progress you make, no matter how incremental it may seem. Every step forward, no matter how small, is a testament to your commitment and resilience.

Remember to be kind and patient with yourself. Recovery is a transformative process that requires time, effort, and self-compassion. Be gentle with your thoughts and emotions, and allow yourself to embrace the journey of healing without judgment.

In addition, surround yourself with a supportive network of individuals who believe in your potential and offer encouragement. Seek out relationships and communities that foster positivity, understanding, and empathy. Their presence will provide you with the strength and support needed to navigate the challenges that may arise.

Lastly, always remember that you are not alone on this path. There are countless individuals who have walked a similar journey and have emerged stronger on the other side. Reach out for help when you need it, whether it's through therapy, support groups, or trusted friends and family members. Lean on the wisdom and guidance of those who have experienced similar struggles and have successfully overcome them.

Believe in yourself, dear reader. You have already taken significant steps towards your recovery, and that in itself is a testament to your resilience and determination. Trust in your ability to face the challenges ahead, knowing that you have the power to shape your own future. Keep moving forward, one step at a time, and know that you have my unwavering support and belief in your journey of transformation and healing.

Something that often goes unacknowledged is the greatness within you. Not everyone takes the time to reflect upon their health and habits, and it is a commendable feat that you have chosen to do so. Your willingness to engage in introspection and evaluate the impact of your choices on your well-being is a testament to your strength and self-awareness.

You should take great pride in this self-reflective journey you have embarked upon. It is an act of courage and personal growth to confront areas of your life that may require change and improvement. By acknowledging the need for change, you have already taken a significant step towards a healthier and more fulfilling existence.

It is important to recognize that reflection alone is not enough. Action is what brings about transformation and positive change. I genuinely hope that you possess the inner strength and determination to not only identify areas of improvement but also take decisive steps towards personal growth and self-betterment.

Believe in your own power to effect change. Trust in your ability to make the necessary adjustments and embrace new habits and behaviors that will enhance your well-being. This journey may not always be easy, but the rewards are immeasurable. Each positive change you make will contribute to your overall growth and happiness.

Embrace the opportunity to evolve into the best version of yourself. Celebrate every milestone, no matter how small, and remember that progress is a continuous journey. Be patient with yourself, as change takes time and effort. Allow room for self-compassion and self-forgiveness along the way, for it is through these acts of kindness towards yourself that you will find the strength to persevere.

Chapter 9: Conclusion

Recap of my journey towards recovery and the lessons you've learned along the way

As we reach the conclusion of this book, it is important to acknowledge the elusive nature of gaming addiction. It can often go unnoticed or be disguised as a mere passion or hobby. We are skilled at convincing ourselves that our actions stem from genuine love and enjoyment rather than from underlying compulsions or urges. Confronting the reality of gaming addiction can be an arduous task. It requires us to peel back the layers of denial and self-deception, to acknowledge that we may indeed have a problem that needs addressing. It is far easier to brush aside any concerns and convince ourselves that everything is fine, rather than facing the uncomfortable truth.

However, true growth and healing begin with self-awareness and honesty. By recognizing the potential presence of addiction in our lives, we open ourselves up to the possibility of positive change. We empower ourselves to break free from the grip of unhealthy habits and patterns.

Taking care of oneself is of utmost importance. It is crucial to consider the well-being of the future version of ourselves —the "you" of tomorrow. What can we do today to support and nurture that person? How can we make choices and take actions that will contribute to a life we genuinely want to live?

Take action towards digital minimalism and addiction recovery

As we reach the conclusion of this book, it becomes evident that gaming addiction is a complex and elusive phenomenon. It has a way of disguising itself, making it difficult to recognize its grip on our lives. We often find ourselves justifying our actions, convincing ourselves that our engagement with games is purely driven by love and enjoyment, rather than a deeper compulsion or inner urge.

Confronting the reality of gaming addiction is not an easy task. It requires us to challenge our own perceptions, confront our habits, and acknowledge the potential harm that excessive gaming can inflict upon our well-being. It is far simpler to deny the existence of a problem, to bury our heads in the sand, and convince ourselves that everything is fine.

However, true growth and personal transformation come from facing our realities head-on. It is through self-reflection and honest introspection that we can begin to dismantle the walls of denial and self-deception. By mustering the courage to acknowledge the presence of gaming addiction in our lives, we open ourselves up to the possibility of change and the opportunity to create a more fulfilling future. Taking care of oneself is of utmost importance in this journey of recovery. It goes beyond the superficial acts of self-care and delves into a deeper understanding of what truly nourishes our mind, body, and soul. Consider the person you aspire to be tomorrow and reflect upon how your actions today can contribute to the well-being of that future self.

Caring for yourself involves making conscious choices that prioritize your long-term happiness and fulfillment. It means recognizing the negative consequences that excessive gaming can have on your relationships, physical health, mental well-being, and personal growth. It requires setting boundaries, finding alternative outlets for relaxation and enjoyment, and investing time and energy in activities that align with your values and aspirations.

Building a life that you truly want to live is a gradual process that requires patience, perseverance, and self-compassion. It is about creating a harmonious balance between your passions, responsibilities, and personal growth. By gradually reducing the hold of gaming addiction and replacing it with meaningful pursuits, you can shape a life that is aligned with your authentic self and brings you genuine fulfillment.

Remember that this journey is not one that you have to embark on alone. Seek support from loved ones, join communities of individuals going through similar challenges, and leverage the wisdom and resources available to you. Surround yourself with individuals who understand and encourage your desire for change, as their support will provide the strength and motivation needed to overcome obstacles along the way.

As we conclude this book, I implore you to take the lessons learned and apply them to your own life. Acknowledge the presence of gaming addiction, challenge the narratives you've created, and make a conscious effort to take care of yourself and build a future that aligns with your true desires. Believe in your own capacity to transform, and trust that every step you take towards recovery brings you closer to a life of authenticity and fulfillment.

May this book serve as a guiding light on your journey to overcome gaming addiction and create a life that truly reflects who you are and what you aspire to be. You have the power to make a lasting change, and I wish you all the strength, resilience, and determination as you navigate the path ahead.

In a world where media inundates us with a constant barrage of games, entertainment, and overstimulation, it is crucial to rise above the noise and seek out experiences that truly make us feel alive. It is all too easy to succumb to the allure of mindless escapism and allow ourselves to drift aimlessly, disconnected from our true passions and purpose.

But we have the power to break free from this cycle of passive consumption and reclaim our lives. We can choose to navigate the sea of distractions with intention and purpose, seeking out activities that ignite our senses, engage our minds, and nourish our souls. Instead of allowing ourselves to be carried away by the currents of mindless entertainment, we can actively participate in the creation of our own meaningful and fulfilling experiences.

Discovering what truly makes us feel alive requires us to step outside of our comfort zones and explore new avenues of interest. It involves embracing the unknown, taking risks, and challenging ourselves to grow. It may be through pursuing a creative passion, engaging in physical activities that invigorate our bodies, or immersing ourselves in the wonders of the natural world. The possibilities are endless.

By consciously choosing to engage in activities that align with our values, ignite our passions, and bring us a sense of purpose, we can break free from the clutches of overstimulation and find genuine fulfillment. Rather than allowing ourselves to be passively entertained, we can become active participants in our own lives, shaping our experiences and creating memories that will truly resonate with us.

It is important to recognize that this journey towards a more meaningful and vibrant existence requires effort and self-reflection. It demands that we question the narratives that society imposes upon us and seek out our own authentic path. It may require us to let go of certain habits or patterns that no longer serve us and make room for new and enriching experiences.

In this pursuit, it is essential to surround ourselves with individuals who support and inspire us. Seek out like-minded individuals who share your desire for a more fulfilling life and who encourage your growth and exploration. Together, you can embark on adventures, exchange ideas, and celebrate the joys of living a life that is purposeful and alive.

In a world that constantly seeks to numb our minds and distract us from what truly matters, we have the power to rise above and choose a different path. Embrace the beauty of living consciously, and let the experiences that truly make you feel alive propel you towards a future filled with vitality, passion, and fulfillment.

www.ingramcontent.com/pod-product-compliance
Lightning Source LLC
LaVergne TN
LVHW052058060326
832903LV00061B/3617